SIMPLICITY LESSONS

ALSO BY LINDA BREEN PIERCE

Choosing Simplicity

Take Back Your Time
(Contributing Author)

SIMPLICITY LESSONS

A 12-STEP GUIDE TO LIVING SIMPLY

Linda Breen Pierce

GALLAGHER PRESS
CARMEL, CALIFORNIA

Attention Organizations, Corporations, Universities, and Community Groups: Quantity discounts are available on bulk purchases of this book for educational, promotional, or fund raising purposes. For information, contact Gallagher Press at PO Box 4136, Carmel, CA 93921 or via Email: info@gallagherpress.com.

The author may be contacted via email at pierce@gallagherpress.com.

PUBLISHER'S CATALOGING-IN-PUBLICATION DATA

Pierce, Linda Breen.
Simplicity Lessons : a 12-step guide to living simply / Linda Breen Pierce. – 1st ed.
p. cm.
Includes bibliographical references and index.
LCCN: 2003091410
ISBN: 0-9672067-9-0

1. Simplicity. 2. Conduct of life. I. Title.
BJ1496.P54 2003 178

First edition

Edited by Hal Zina Bennett
Book cover design: Hartmann Design Group
Book interior design and composition: John Reinhardt Book Design

Printed and bound in the United States of America

10 9 8 7 6 5 4 3 2 1

I dedicate this book to the
villagers of Keur Saloum Diané, Senegal, West Africa.
You taught me my first
and most profound lessons in simplicity.

Acknowledgments

Many have offered support in the creation of this book. I would especially like to acknowledge the following:

- To the Monterey Peninsula simplicity study group who offered their enthusiasm and commitment for a trial run of the first draft of this book: Diane Crow, Charles Crow, Cathy Gribas, Mabelle Lernoud, Barbee Swofford, Kathy Warthan, Joan Zielinski, and John Zielinski. Many thanks for the heartwarming exchanges, good food, and great fun.
- To Jennifer Gregan-Paxton, Tim Kasser, Nikki Nedeff, and Susan Posch, each of whom critiqued portions of the manuscript. Your insights and suggestions were invaluable. Thank you so much for your generosity.
- To Hal Zina Bennett, my steadfast editor. Once again, you saved my butt. You are a jewel.
- To my dear friend, Sharon Miller, who patiently and graciously read every word of the manuscript with her keen eyes and sharp wit. You have kept me laughing over these many years, for which I'm grateful.
- To my fellow hikers, the Glamazons: Susan Boehlert, Bonnie Brooks, Nancy Callahan, Ruth Carter, Mardo Collins, Amelia Craig, Rita Dalessio, Sheila Dixon, Terry Hallock, Christy Herman, Linda Holland, Nikki Nedeff, and Robin Sutherlin. Thank you for your friendship and support. Our weekly hikes provide a rejuvenating break from the rigors of the writing life.
- To LJ Holland, my soul-mate in this life of writing. Our weekly meetings have kept me on track. I am so grateful for your friendship, your sense of humor, and your insistence that I occasionally upgrade my wardrobe.
- To my husband, Jim Pierce, for all your support—financially, emotionally, and in all the little and big things you do for me. I hope to repay you someday, perhaps in heaven.

Contents

INTRODUCTION

MY WISH FOR YOU

Have you ever been inspired by a book but then failed to integrate what you learned into your life? I have. For example, when I read books on writing I often experience *aha* moments throughout, but that doesn't mean I can turn those insights into great prose. There was, however, one notable exception in my experience. And that was *The Artist's Way* by Julia Cameron. In her book, Cameron offers enlightened wisdom on the creative process. She describes the spiritual dimension in creating art in a way that spoke to my heart. But she did something else. She asked me, as a reader of her book, to step up to the plate and account for my own creative process. She asked me questions that were difficult and sometimes uncomfortable for me to answer. She suggested practices and tasks for me to complete. She kept asking me (dang!) how I did the previous week on my assignments.

When I finished reading (or perhaps I should say *living*), *The Artist's Way*, I owned the *aha* moments I felt. They were now a part of my life. For years now, I have followed the suggested practice of writing the *morning pages* Cameron recommends to keep your creativity flowing. They are still working their wonders.

In fact, I used those creative practices to produce my first book, *Choosing Simplicity*, which features the real life stories of people who have simplified their lives. *Choosing Simplicity* is based on my three-year study of over 200 people from 40 states and eight countries. Observing others can be an effective way to learn about something. Reading about others' challenges and successes can also give us support and motivation to continue on our own journeys.

It is my hope with this book to help you go beyond being enlightened and inspired about the benefits and challenges of living more simply. I want you to actually experience it in your life—to feel the immense joy and fulfillment that simplicity brings. Like *The Artist's Way* did for me, I hope to offer you a tool that will allow you to take whatever you learn from this book and make it an integral part of your life. I want to give you the means to continue on your path of simplicity for years after you read this book. In this book, I will ask you to do the work that's required to make this happen.

Simplicity touches our lives on many levels, from the deeply personal (your sense of self, your inner world) to the global issues of environmental sustainability and social justice. In this book, we will explore how simplicity can improve our lives as individuals and the lives of those in our family, our local community, our country, and our world.

Whether you work with this book alone, with a partner, or as a participant in a simplicity study group, I hope it will be a challenging and exciting adventure for you.

Everything should be made as simple as possible, but not simpler.

Albert Einstein

WHAT INSPIRED THIS BOOK

Necessity is the mother of invention and occasionally of books. It certainly inspired this book. It all started in February of 2002, when I facilitated a simplicity workshop in my local community. At the end of the workshop, 20 people expressed interest in exploring simplicity in greater depth. Many were interested in a simplicity study group, a small group of people who meet for 10 to 12 sessions to discuss how they can live more simply. Others could not participate due to conflicting schedules or distant locations.

I conducted an orientation meeting for those interested in a study group. We immediately faced our first challenge: what were we going to talk about? After all, voluntary simplicity—living consciously and deliberately, focusing on what you truly need or genuinely cherish—is a huge topic, covering diverse areas such as the stuff cluttering our lives, time, money, work, and caring for the earth.

And which of the available simplicity study books and guides would be our best choice? A simplicity study guide provides the structure and suggestions for discussion for the group's sessions. Many of the existing guides focus on several of the topics we wanted to explore, but no single one covered the full scope of our interests. The group's enthusiasm was strong; we wanted to tackle it all. It was in response to this need that I decided to write this book. Our local study group served as my guinea pigs to test out the lessons included in this book.

I was also concerned about the people who could not join the group, but who still wanted to explore simplicity in depth. While a group learning environment can provide a powerful, inspirational experience and a much-needed sense of community, some people prefer the solo route. Sometimes it's their only option. Their schedules or family obligations make it impractical to participate in the group sessions, or they cannot find others (or don't want to search for them) in their community to join them. In response to this need, I've designed this book to be used either by groups or by individuals working alone.

I had yet another reason to write this book. It has been three years since my book, *Choosing Simplicity*, was published. Since its publication, I have given keynote speeches and workshops on simplicity in the United States and Europe. I worked with Vicki Robin, Duane Elgin, Cecile Andrews, John de Graaf, and other simplicity advocates to organize *The Simplicity Forum*, an innovative think-tank and activist group of leaders in the simplicity movement. Collectively, there has been substantial brainstorming, learning, and refinement of ideas taking place. In this book, I hope to draw from that learning process to provide a clear and concise roadmap for those who seek to bring simplicity into their lives.

Simplicity is an acquired taste. Mankind, left free, instinctively complicates life.

Katharine Fullerton Gerould

WHO SHOULD READ THIS BOOK

I wrote this book for both the curious and the committed. Perhaps you are new to this area or have signed up for a class on the subject. Others may approach the subject from a more practical view; they are already sold on the concept and are eager to integrate simplicity principles into their lives.

This book may be used by individuals working alone, two people working together, classes in an educational setting, or by community groups who meet together to share the learning process. It is relevant for many segments of society, including college students, working people, full-time parents, single adults, and those who are retired or financially independent. While a life of simplicity may appear vastly different from one person to the next, or at different stages in one person's life, the overall principles are the same.

Tell me, and I'll forget. Show me, and I may not remember. Involve me, and I'll understand.

Native American Saying

HOW TO USE THIS BOOK

Simplicity touches almost every aspect of our lives—work, relationships, leisure, spirituality, health, money, material possessions, housing, transportation, community, and environmental issues, to name a few. While a commitment to live simply can be daunting, its rewards, as you'll learn in this book, are substantial.

In this book, you will be called on to define a life of simplicity unique to you and your family. You have inside yourself the intuitive knowledge of how you can best live more simply. My role is simply to help you access that knowledge. I purposely left space on each page for you to record your reactions—mark it up, make it real! Feel free to disagree with me; sarcasm and humor are welcome. Note also the points that speak to your heart.

This book breaks the subject of simplicity into manageable pieces—not exactly bite-sized, but sufficiently distinct to digest without feeling overwhelmed. Each lesson features one or two interrelated topics. You will read a general discussion of the topic, followed by *lesson assignments*—questions and exercises for you to review and complete. It is a good idea to read the general discussion portion first, let it percolate in your subconscious for a few days, and then apply yourself to the questions and exercises. Take notes of your responses to later share with others in your group, or if you are working by yourself, write your responses in a journal (see *Individuals Working Alone* below).

After you complete the group session or individual journal session, you are invited to undertake one or more *lifework assignments* designed to help you further integrate the lesson into your life. These tasks may require some time and effort. If you take notes on your progress periodically, it will motivate you to continue. If you are a member of a group, feel free to share your progress with the group during the Check-in procedure in subsequent lessons (see Appendix B).

You may also want to do further study on your own by referring to the Recommended Resources at the end of each lesson. Throughout the book, I refer to web sites and resources to be found on the Internet. If you don't have a computer with Internet access, you are likely to find one in a public library or Internet café.

Finally, there is an *Annual Check-up* for each lesson, consisting of questions to contemplate and actions to take for the following year. After you complete each lesson, make a note in your calendar for one year later to review the Annual Check-up section.

The following sections describe various ways to use this book—as a member of a study group or circle, working with one other person, or working alone.

THE STUDY CIRCLE

According to the Study Circles Resource Center, "a study circle is a group of 8 to 12 people from different backgrounds and viewpoints who meet several times to talk about an issue. In a study circle, everyone has an equal voice, and people try to understand each other's views. They do not have to agree with each other. The idea is to share concerns and look for ways to make things better. A facilitator helps the group focus on different views and makes sure the discussion goes well."

A little simplification would be the first step toward rational living, I think.

Eleanor Roosevelt

The concept of study circles is not new. They were used by the Chautauqua movement in the late 19th century. Subsequently, Sweden adopted study circles as a popular form of lifelong education. Currently in the United States there are study circles focusing on a wide range of topics including simplicity, race, education, neighborhoods, criminal justice, growth, and youth violence.

Cecile Andrews, author of *Circle of Simplicity*, is known for introducing the study circle form of learning to the field of simplicity. Today, there are hundreds if not thousands of simplicity study circles throughout North America.[1] The terms *simplicity discussion group* and *simplicity study group* are used interchangeably to describe the simplicity study circle.

The benefits of participating in a simplicity study group are many. First, it offers participants a supportive environment to explore a way of life that is not always valued by mainstream culture. Second, learning potential is multiplied by group interaction, especially in the area of problem solving. For example, if you are striving to cut back your work hours to spend more time on other important priorities, eight heads working together are often better than struggling on your own. Finally, in our community-deprived culture, a simplicity study group provides a peer group, a *tribe* of sorts with which we can identify.

Finding or starting a simplicity study group is not difficult. Even in the smallest communities, there are generally 8 to 12 people who would be interested in participating. The Appendixes A through D provide all the information you need to start a group.

WORKING WITH A PARTNER

You create simplicity by chipping away at the unreal, the useless, and the meaningless until, like Michaelangelo's David, you are left with a life that is breathtakingly beautiful.

Vicki Robin

Perhaps you don't want to participate in a group, but you have a friend who is interested in learning more about simplicity. Working with even one other person has benefits. Just establishing a time and place for regular meetings will encourage you to do the work in this guide. When you listen to each other's responses to the questions and exercises, you act as a witness for the other, offering validation just by listening. Working together, you create an environment of support, encouragement, and fruitful brainstorming. You and your partner can follow the same procedures outlined for group sessions (see Appendixes A and B).

INDIVIDUALS WORKING ALONE

You don't need to be a member of a group to benefit from this study guide. Working alone, you can do the suggested exercises at the end of each lesson. Then, instead of sharing your thoughts in a group, you will record your responses in a journal or on your computer. It is important to record your thoughts in some fashion rather than just allowing them to roam about in the caverns of your mind. Recording your thoughts is a way of *catching* them, of making them real. Otherwise, they have a tendency to be vague and fleeting, making it difficult to build on them.

If you're not comfortable with writing as a way of talking to yourself, you can speak into a tape recorder instead. Imagine yourself sharing your thoughts with a very close friend or significant other. At the end of the course, you will have a series of tapes of your work. Like a written journal, it can be helpful to listen to these tapes at some point in the future.

A MESSAGE TO COLLEGE STUDENTS AND YOUNG ADULTS

I have a special place in my heart for young adults. This stems in part from the fact that I learned my most dramatic lessons in simplicity during the three months I lived in a bush village in Senegal, West Africa, when I was 20 years old. That experience had a profound impact on my life during the decades to follow. If I could grant you any wish, it would be to spend a few months in a less industrialized country. It could give you a perspective on life that would influence every aspect of your future.

As a young adult, you have the freedom and idealism to create your life from scratch—what work you will do, where to live, how to live, what's most important to you. As we age, we become less facile at learning and changing. For example, a four-year old will learn a second language more easily and quickly than a 40-year old. The same holds true for simplicity. The sooner you start on this journey, the less you will have to unlearn.

A dreamer—you know—it's a mind that looks over the edges of things.

Mary O'Hara

I hope with this book to offer you an alternative to the work-and-spend treadmill that characterizes the mainstream of North American culture. It is also becoming increasingly clear that the future of the earth and quality of life to be experienced by all peoples depends on you. Whatever choices you make in your life will greatly affect how coming generations will live.

As a student you can use this guide individually, as a member of an informal study group on campus, or even in a course on voluntary simplicity or related subjects. Since this guide is also for the general public, you might find some portions of the lessons to be irrelevant to you right now. For example, if you are a typical college student, you are unlikely to have a large home filled with expensive furnishings and screaming children, a full-time job, and a long commute. But you do live somewhere, have to transport yourself somehow, and still have plenty of things in your life. Most of what is in this book will have relevance to you right now.

As a college student, you will likely want to expand your reading to include some of the recommended books and resources at the end of each lesson. If you would like to see the subject of voluntary simplicity integrated into your college curriculum, ask your teachers to review the *Manual for University and College Professors* for this text. It can be found on the Gallagher Press web site [www.gallagherpress.com] under the heading, *Current Releases*.

A MESSAGE TO PEOPLE WHO LIVE OUTSIDE NORTH AMERICA

We are all more blind to what we have than to what we have not.

Audre Lorde

Even though I am a dual citizen of Ireland and the United States, I have lived most of my life in the United States. Consequently, this book is necessarily written from an American point of view. However, having spent time in Europe, I know that the life questions confronting North Americans are not unique. While cultures and values may vary from country to country, the concepts discussed in this book are universal.

As for citizens of less-industrialized countries who aspire to the North American way of life, this book will illustrate how the so-called American dream does not always deliver what it promises. You will learn that there is a substantial price to be paid for our materialistic emphasis. Hopefully, this book will guide you on which aspects of the American dream are worth working for and which are not. You can then avoid making the same mistake as many North Americans who equate a very high standard of living on a material plane with a high-quality life.

And now let's get to work!

LESSON 1

WHY SIMPLIFY?

WHAT'S WRONG WITH THIS PICTURE?

As a nation, the United States has doubled its living standards in the last 50 years. The average home size has expanded from 1,100 square feet to 2,300 square feet, while family sizes have decreased.[1] Per capita spending has tripled from $6,800 to over $24,000 per year (inflated adjusted).[2] At no other time in history have Americans experienced such a long ride of *high living*. We enjoy the fruits of an economy that provides not only our basic needs for food, clothing, and shelter but also seemingly limitless luxuries.

If you doubt this, spend some time in other countries; the bountiful and luxurious nature of America's standard of living will be quite apparent. It's not that we don't have real poverty in this country—we do. But the vast majority of people in the United States maintain a standard of living that far exceeds that of other countries. Yet, notwithstanding such economic growth and material abundance, the percentage of Americans who rate themselves as "very happy" has decreased since the 1950's.[3]

At this point in time, Americans are seriously confused. According to *The Harvard Group* 1995 report, *Yearning for Balance*, Americans feel their priorities are "out of whack, that materialism, greed, and selfishness increasingly dominate American life, crowding out a more meaningful set of values centered on family, responsibility, and community." Still, Americans are ambivalent about what to do. While we are aware that our deepest aspirations are nonmaterial in nature, we feel attached to our material comforts and do not want to give them up.

In addition to our relative material wealth, we Americans are quite proud of our productivity and efficiency. Not only are our businesses excellent models of bigger, better, and faster, our personal lives are time management marvels. It is astounding what we accomplish with our computers, cell phones, voice mail, calendar systems, household appliances, and automobiles. With all this technological support, we maintain schedules that would exhaust our great grandparents just to hear about.

So, what's wrong with this picture? A little voice inside many of us whines, "I have a nice home, great family, good health, a decent job—how come I'm not happy? Something is just not right."

For starters, let's look at our work lives. During the last 50 years, we have added a full month to our annual work hours.[4] In 1997, the United States had the dubious distinction of surpassing Japan for the highest number of hours worked (based on averages) in the industrial world.[5]

Excessive work hours seem to go hand in hand with runaway spending and before you know it, we feel trapped on a seemingly endless work-and-spend treadmill. As a culture, we define success as wealth, power, and status. Unfortunately, beyond the level of moderate material means, these assets don't give us the sense of well-being we seek. Research studies on happiness tell us that once basic material needs are met, the key indicators of happiness are relationships, community, meaningful work or purpose, spirituality, and connection with nature.[6]

The great disadvantage of being in a rat race is that it is humiliating. The competitors in a rat race are, by definition, rodents.

Margaret Halsey

We are living the American dream gone amuck. We work and spend, yet neglect the softer, soulful aspects of life. However, the intuitive knowledge that our deepest aspirations are nonmaterial in nature is leading many people to simplify their lives. A growing number of North Americans have said, "Enough!" They reject the cultural conditioning that more and bigger are always better. For these people, personal freedom, enhanced relationships, a deeper spirituality, and meaningful work have replaced the quest for ever-increasing wealth and status.

Another major influence leading people to simplify is their concern for the earth. While environmentalists have expressed concern for decades, business and political leaders around the world now acknowledge that our planet cannot survive to the end of the 21st century if we continue on the current path of resource utilization and waste generation.

As Americans, we need to face that fact that even though we comprise less than five percent of the world's population, we are responsible for nearly 25 percent of global carbon emissions.[7] One child born in North America consumes 30 to 50 times more resources during his lifetime than a child born in a developing country.[8] We will consider the environmental impact of our lifestyles in more detail as we complete the lessons in this book.

VOLUNTARY SIMPLICITY

I believe that living simply greatly enhances quality of life for individuals and families, strengthens communities and societies, and contributes to the earth's present and future health. Voluntary simplicity or simple living means living consciously and deliberately, focusing on what you truly need or genuinely cherish. This concept relates not only to material possessions but also to work, relationships, how we spend our leisure time, and the choices we make that impact the earth and other people. Living simply is not about rejecting the material comforts in life, but it does involve unburdening our lives, living more lightly with fewer distractions.

Voluntary simplicity means going fewer places in one day rather than more, doing less so I can do more, acquiring less so I can have more.

Jon Kabat-Zinn

Voluntary is a key element of the philosophy of simple living. Living without adequate food, shelter, clothing, and medical care is not simple living. Nor is it voluntary simplicity; it is involuntary poverty.

Some people associate voluntary simplicity with living in the country on next to nothing, growing your own food and relying on the sun for energy, or perhaps living in a tiny apartment in the city with no funds for urban pleasures. In fact, only a small percentage of people who live simply choose such frugal lifestyles. Most are ordinary people with families and regular jobs. They live in cities, suburbs, and small towns.

The concept of simple living is nothing new or unique to this time in history. The principles of simplicity are found in the work of early Greek philosophers and in many religions. In *The Simple Life*, historian David E. Shi traces the history of simplicity movements during the last 500 years. It appears that simplicity movements arise in cycles, alternating with periods of excess. When societies experience prolonged bouts of excess, there comes a time when people yearn to return to a simpler life. We are at that point now in North America.

Simplicity does not prescribe a set of rigid rules. It is more a mindset, a way of looking at life, a commitment to live consciously and deliberately. Simple living is not the same thing as easy living. It's not that easy to figure out what you really need or cherish and then make it happen. Sometimes it's far from easy, but it is deeply satisfying, offering opportunities for deep joy, inner peace, and fulfillment.

Simplicity is first and foremost an inside job. For many people, it involves a process of inner growth—spending time in quiet reflection, often over a number of months or years—to develop their unique version of simplicity. In its essence, simplicity is about being who you really are, living a life designed by you rather than one dictated by society. And it is a life-long journey. What may be a simple life for you today might look radically different in 10 years.

To live fully, outwardly and inwardly, not to ignore external reality for the sake of the inner life, or the reverse—that's quite a task.

Etty Hillesum

Some people are interested in simplicity for those values that are primarily *self-directed*—more time, personal freedom, reduced stress, a slower pace of life, control of money, less stuff to maintain, fulfilling work, passion and purpose in life, joyful relationships, deeper spirituality, better health, and a connection with nature. Others are motivated more by *other-directed* values—protecting the earth's resources, remedying social injustice, serving the community, and caring for others.

Some critics of the voluntary simplicity movement claim that people who live simply are selfish and self-centered, focusing on their personal fulfillment and happiness rather than the concerns of the world. In fact, while many people first approach simplicity with an interest in *self-directed* values, they soon develop *other-directed* values. An almost magical transformation takes place.

It happens on two levels: the external and internal. Obviously, as people slow down the pace of their lives, they have more time and energy to engage in earth-friendly practices and to be of service to others. But something else takes place on an internal level. When we remove the material and lifestyle clutter from our lives, we seem to open up a space within ourselves for deep caring—caring for the earth, other people, future generations, and life on the planet. Simplicity brings out the best in humanity. It facilitates a spiritual awakening in which we experience our connection to other people and nature. Once that happens, the deep caring follows. Gradually, we embody more of the *other-directed* values as we discover that our personal happiness and fulfillment depend on it.

In summary, simplicity helps people fulfill their deepest needs and aspirations, which in turn leads them to behave in ways that make this world a better place. Specific lifestyles of simplicity will vary enormously because what a person needs or cherishes is a subjective determination. Nonetheless, I have observed the following common lifestyle patterns in people who live simply:

1. Limiting material possessions to what is needed and/or cherished.
2. Meaningful work, whether paid or volunteer, ideally spending no more than 30 hours per week (in order to make time for items # 3 to 12, below).
3. Quality relationships with friends and family.
4. Joyful and pleasurable leisure activities.
5. A conscious and comfortable relationship with money.
6. Connection to community, but not necessarily in formal organizations.
7. Sustainable consumption practices.
8. Healthy living practices, including exercise, adequate sleep, and nutritious food.
9. Practices that foster personal growth, an inner life, or spirituality, such as yoga, meditation, prayer, religious ceremonies, journal writing, and spiritually-related reading.
10. Connection to nature—delighting in spending time in nature regularly.
11. Aesthetic beauty in personal environment.
12. Living in harmony with values and integrity.

There are no new ideas.
There are only new ways
of making them felt.

Audre Lorde

Many of the items on this list overlap. For example, walking in nature gives you a sense of connection with the earth and benefits both your health and your soul. Parenting is both a form of meaningful work and the foundation for quality family relationships.

As citizens of democratic nations, we have enormous freedom and choice about how to live. We can choose to live simply. For example, thousands of families have proved that it is indeed possible to live well on one income in North America.

Many who are living simply work part-time, earning money doing what they love. With creativity, planning, and patience, you can work less, want less, and spend less to gain a life of inner peace and fulfillment.

However, if you live in North America (or to some extent in any industrialized country), you will need courage, a high level of self-esteem, and the ability to be a self-starter. You will be rowing upstream against the current of mainstream culture. Our governmental, corporate, and social institutions encourage us to earn as much money as we can, acquire a never-ending supply of luxuries, and work to exhaustion. Career and material success are the standard barometers of status in our society.

Courage can't see around corners, but goes around them anyway.

Mignon McLaughlin

While thousands of people have proved you can carve out a life of simplicity in North America, obviously it would be much easier if social and public policies favored a simple, high-quality life for all. Therefore, as we review each lesson in this book, we will consider not only what we can do individually but also what social and public policies would create a more simplicity-friendly society.

LESSON ASSIGNMENTS

Note: if you are a member of a study group, you would normally break up into smaller groups to review the lesson assignments (see Appendix B). However, for this first lesson, the entire group should remain together to discuss the following questions. It will give you a great start in getting to know each other.

1. What does simple living or voluntary simplicity mean to you? How would you define it?
2. What is it about your life right now that attracts you to simplicity?
3. Have you experimented with simplifying your life in some ways? What were the results?
4. Can you imagine what your ideal life of simplicity would look like? Describe it in as much detail as you can.

LIFEWORK ASSIGNMENTS

There are no specific lifework assignments for this lesson other than to complete the remaining lessons in this book.

ANNUAL CHECK-UP

1. Compare your life now with your life one year ago. Do you feel more or less joy, fulfillment, and inner peace? Describe briefly any major changes in your life. You will have an opportunity to reflect more specifically on those changes in the subsequent lessons to follow.
2. If you completed this course as an individual working alone, you may want to start or join a simplicity study group as part of your annual review of the subsequent lessons in this book. If you completed this course as a member of a group, you may want to participate in a less structured discussion group on simplicity (see *Epilogue, Where Do We Go From Here?* for ideas for ongoing groups).
3. Proceed to review the annual check-up suggestions for each subsequent lesson.

RECOMMENDED RESOURCES

The following books and other resources will give you a broad overview of voluntary simplicity. Many of them include discussion of the topics in the subsequent lessons in this book. Most of the books are considered classics in this field.

BOOKS

Affluenza: The All-Consuming Epidemic by John de Graaf, David Wann, Thomas H. Naylor (San Francisco: Berrett-Koehler, 2001). Explores the personal, social, economic, and environmental costs of overconsumption in North America. Suggests strategies for rebuilding families and communities, respecting the earth, and restoring personal health and sanity in a world suffering from excess.

Choosing Simplicity: Real People Finding Peace and Fulfillment in a Complex World by Linda Breen Pierce (Carmel, CA: Gallagher Press, 2000). Features wide range of real life stories of people who have simplified their lives. Offers guidance on how to integrate lessons derived from these diversified life examples.

Circle of Simplicity: Return to the Good Life by Cecile Andrews (New York: Harper Collins, 1997). Foremost leader in the development of voluntary simplicity study circles explores themes integral to simplicity, including finding your passion, living authentically, connecting with community, and spirituality. Includes guide for forming study circle.

Gift From the Sea by Anne Morrow Lindbergh (New York: Pantheon Books, Reissued 1991). Classic memoir of voluntary simplicity. Rumination of author's life and the values of simplicity written during author's stay at the seashore. Originally written in 1955, still relevant today.

The Good Life: Helen and Scott Nearing's Sixty Years of Self-Sufficient Living by Scott Nearing and Helen Nearing (New York: Schocken Books, Reprinted 1990). Classic text of homesteading lifestyle. Detailed description of authors' experience living in rural Vermont, complete with specific information on food and shelter. Authors promote value of substantial leisure time engaged in reading, music, and conversation.

Graceful Simplicity: Toward a Philosophy and Politics of Simple Living by Jerome M. Segal (New York: Henry Holt, 1999). Philosopher and political activist contends that the grass roots, self-help approach to simple living is inadequate to effectuate lasting changes in our culture. Proposes political and social changes to our cultural and financial institutions.

A Reasonable Life: Toward a Simpler, Secure, More Humane Existence by Ferenc Maté (Pflugerville, TX: Albatross Publishing, 2nd edition, 2000). Presents a compelling, witty, radical and passionate diatribe on the state of American society, with corresponding suggestions on how to turn our world back right-side-up.

The Simple Life: Plain Living and High Thinking in American Culture by David E. Shi (Athens, GA: University of Georgia Press, Reprinted 2001). Comprehensive historical review of various simplicity movements from the 17th to 20th centuries, written by scholar and researcher of intellectual history.

The Simple Living Guide: A Sourcebook for Less Stressful, More Joyful Living by Janet Luhrs (New York: Broadway Books, 1997). Comprehensive guide on various aspects of simple living, including time, money, inner simplicity, work, simple pleasures and romance, virtues, families, holidays, cooking and nutrition, health and exercise, housing, clutter, gardening and travel.

Simpler Living, Compassionate Life: A Christian Perspective by Michael Schut, editor (Denver, CO: Living the Good News, 1999). Diversified collection of essays written by experts in the simplicity movement offers excellent overview of the principles of voluntary simplicity.

Simplicity: Notes, Stories and Exercises for Developing Unimaginable Wealth by Mark A. Burch (Gabriola Island, B.C.: New Society Publishers, 1995). Explores the spiritual nature of voluntary simplicity, mindfulness, direct personal involvement in everyday living, ecological issues such as reducing waste and consumption, sustainable development, and greater equitable distribution of the world's wealth and resources.

Simplify Your Life: 100 Ways to Slow Down and Enjoy the Things That Really Matter by Elaine St. James (New York: Hyperion, 1994). Classic popular bestseller offering practical tips on simplifying in the areas of career, household, health, social, finance, and personal affairs.

The Value of Voluntary Simplicity by Richard Gregg (Wallingford, PA: Pendle Hill, 1936). Philosophical essay on the need and benefits of living more simply. Still relevant for the 21st century. Author coined term "voluntary simplicity."

Voluntary Simplicity: Toward a Way of Life that is Outwardly Simple, Inwardly Rich by Duane Elgin (New York: Quill, Revised 1993). Classic seminal text for the modern voluntary simplicity movement. Discusses implications of voluntary simplicity from individual and societal/global points of view.

Walden and Other Writings by Henry David Thoreau (New York: Modern Library, 2000). Classic simplicity tome by the *father* of simplicity. Reveals author's experience of living on Walden Pond for two years in the nineteenth century. Inspirational, providing a depth of meaning to the quest for simplicity.

MISCELLANEOUS

The Simple Living Network [www.simpleliving.net] is an excellent, comprehensive web site on simple living. Dave Wampler, founder of The Simple Living Network, edits and publishes a free email newsletter. This web site is a fountain of simplicity resources. You can also purchase most of the books that are mentioned in this book from The Simple Living Network.

The Simplicity Resource Guide [www.gallagherpress.com/pierce] is written and maintained by Linda Breen Pierce, author of this book. It features book reviews, articles, and links to related sites.

Seeds of Simplicity [www.seedsofsimplicity.org] is a national, non-profit membership organization for the general public centered on voluntary simplicity. It sponsors the Simplicity Circles Project, directed by Cecile Andrews, author of *Circle of Simplicity*.

The New Road Map Foundation [www.newroadmap.org] is a not-for-profit, all volunteer organization that provides numerous resources, including books, audio tapes, study guides and pamphlets, relating to financial integrity, simple living, and preserving the earth's resources.

Simple Living Oasis [www.simpleliving.com], a quarterly journal edited by Janet Luhrs, author of *The Simple Living Guide*, offers tips, tools, and inspiration to those who want to live simply.

NOTE: *Additions and updates to these resources can be found on The Simplicity Resource Guide at www.gallagherpress.com/pierce.*

LESSON 2

Do You Own Your Stuff Or Does It Own You?

HOW MUCH IS ENOUGH?

The stand-up comedian George Carlin performs a wonderfully entertaining routine called "A Place for My Stuff." Dave Barry, a nationally syndicated columnist and author, has written many humorous lines about the stuff in our lives. We often laugh or roll our eyes when this subject comes up. We giggle knowingly in recognition of the love/hate relationship we have with our material possessions.

In North America, we *really* love our stuff. So much so that the Mall of America—a shopping mall in Minnesota of 4.2 million square feet, large enough to house 32 Boeing 747s— attracts more visitors annually than Disney World, Graceland, and the Grand Canyon combined. A 1997 study indicated that the Mall of America was the most visited destination for U.S. travelers.[1]

As attached as we are to our stuff, we also feel it has a life of its own. It seems to creep into our homes through invisible cracks in windows and doors (not even weather stripping will keep it out), filling every nook and cranny, every cupboard, closet, and drawer. When we move to a new home, we are forced to come face to face with our stuff. Shocked to see how much we have, we wonder where it all came from.

Materialism is an emotionally loaded word. It is often associated with disapproval, guilt, or a sense of justification. Some people who value a highly materialistic lifestyle think, "What is so wrong with materialism? If I work hard and can afford luxuries, why not indulge in them?" Others who place a high value on materialism would not admit it publicly. While our lifestyles indicate otherwise, it is generally not acceptable to say that you value materialism as much as family relationships, integrity, or community service.

In fact, there is nothing wrong with materialism *per se*. Simplicity is not about deprivation. To the contrary, it is about living with enough—enough material goods, enough meaningful work, enough relationship and community, enough connection with nature, enough of an inner life. Unfortunately, the quest for a highly materialistic lifestyle often interferes with meeting our nonmaterial needs. If we fill our lives with working and spending, we have little time, energy, or peace of mind for these deeper, less tangible yearnings.

Our task, then, is to determine how much is enough. How much stuff can we enjoy without screwing up the rest of our lives? The answer is simple in concept and incredibly complex in practice. At a minimum, we should have what we need to meet our basic physical needs—clean water, food, shelter, and clothing. Ideally, we would also have those material things we genuinely cherish, which of course will vary considerably from person to person.

We are constantly seeking more only to discover that more is never enough.

Vicki Robin

Figuring out what we need or cherish can be challenging. Sometimes we unconsciously seek material goods to compensate for unmet nonmaterial needs. For example, some people shop to relieve stress, as a treat to counter the dissatisfaction in their lives. Others amass possessions to enhance their sense of self-worth, believing that what they own reflects their status in society.

It's true that buying something new can be exciting and relieve stress or boredom, but often that excitement is short-lived. Once the thrill wears off, we seek another fix, another shopping high, and the cycle continues. We seem to be genetically programmed to always want more. Most of us need to work hard to pay for our spending. Working excessively generates stress and dissatisfaction, for which we seek relief, often in the form of spending more money. Welcome to the work-and-spend treadmill.

In North America, it's easy to be seduced by the material abundance available to us. From a very early age, we are encouraged by corporate advertisers to seek happiness in our possessions. Here is a story taken from my book, *Choosing Simplicity*, which illustrates the point:

> My girlfriend's hubby bought a $3,000 big screen TV. When I asked if a $3,000 TV is that much better than a $2,000 TV or a $1,000 TV, she replied, "Well, John says that in a couple years when he's ready to upgrade, he will get a much better trade-in price." I asked, "Do you mean to tell me that in a couple short years he will no longer be satisfied with a $3,000

TV?" It just hit me that there is something seriously wrong with a society in which people are going to bed hungry and sick, yet some of us are buying $3,000 TVs and planning to be dissatisfied with them very soon.

Of course, we need some material goods to live comfortably. Our possessions can also be a source of beauty and inspiration to us. This was recognized by the proponents of the simplicity movement that emerged at the beginning of the 20th century. That movement was deeply rooted in aestheticism—valuing well-crafted items of great beauty. Likewise, today's simplicity movement recognizes the aesthetic and functional benefits of material goods. There is nothing about simplicity that values an ugly, stiff, uncomfortable couch. Some people associate simplicity with the concept of less is more, but in fact, it is not always so.

How much is enough? That's the question we need to grapple with, and it will be with us for the rest of our lives. As our interests and lifestyles change over time, so will the answer to this question. We can start to solve this puzzle by examining our possessions at this time in our lives. The assignments at the end of this lesson will get us started.

All advertising tells lies, but there are little lies and there are big lies. Little lie: this beer tastes great. Big lie: this beer makes you great.

Leslie Savan

THE COSTLY INTANGIBLES OF MATERIAL POSSESSIONS

Let's consider the life energy that goes into our possessions. First, we need to earn money to pay for goods, although sometimes we defer this step by taking on credit card debt. While work can be fulfilling and enjoyable in its own right, too many of us feel we are working primarily to pay the bills.

Next comes the research phase. If we are buying more than a loaf of bread, we are inclined to do substantial research on the voluminous choices we have today. The Internet has expanded our opportunities to investigate even further. Making a decision becomes increasingly overwhelming. It's a price we pay for this abundance of information. Then, we invest more time and energy to actually purchase the desired items.

Next we deal with insurance and maintenance issues. We

invest time and money to insure our belongings, separately or collectively. Some of us worry about our valuables when we leave our home unattended for several weeks. Maintaining our possessions can also drain us physically and mentally. We either do it ourselves or hire someone else to do it. Even if you are rich, it takes time to select, supervise, and sometimes discharge the people who service your property and possessions.

And finally, the disposition phase—selling or giving away those things we no longer want. Our tastes change. We move to a new home, and our old furniture doesn't fit. We want new furniture, new clothes, or a new car. It's relatively easy to put certain things in a box and donate them to a charity, but some things cost too much to let go of that easily. How about the stationary bicycle you bought for $1,000 and used a total of six times? How easy is it to let go of that? How often do we hold on to things in disrepair, believing we will someday figure out a way to fix them? What about the outmoded computer that no one wants? We shudder at placing it in a landfill. Clearly, a great deal of energy goes into disposing unwanted goods.

Civilization is a limitless multiplication of unnecessary necessaries.

Mark Twain

There is also a psychic cost to possessing things that are unimportant to you. Even if you have room to display or store these items, their presence still intrudes on your peace of mind. Our minds are constantly stimulated by our physical environment. If we surround ourselves with stuff we don't value, we subject our minds to a certain level of chaos, which interferes with our ability to focus on more meaningful aspects of life. Inevitably, people who let go of unvalued possessions report an expansive feeling of freedom and lightness.

Philosophers as far back as Plato and Aristotle have reflected on the seemingly innate desire of humans to possess, to own, to dominate the physical world. Where does this desire come from? Perhaps it's a fear of deprivation, a fear of not having enough. Perhaps the dialogue in our subconscious minds goes something like this: "If I own something, no one can take it away from me. I'm afraid if they did take it away, it would be lost forever, and I would feel deprived for the rest of my life!" My mind plays this trick when I attend a party with excellent food or especially yummy brownies or fudge. I eat as if there will never be delicious food in my life again.

All the physical and emotional energy you devote to the care and feeding of your possessions is time not spent on more rewarding endeavors involving relationships, fulfilling work, creative pursuits, community service, and spending time in nature. It's not a question of denying yourself material pleasures. Rather, the goal is to make sure your material desires don't crowd out nonmaterial pleasures and satisfaction.

KNOW THYSELF — LOOK AT YOUR STUFF

We can learn so much about ourselves by looking at our possessions—how and why we acquired them, what they mean to us, why we still have them. Take clothing for example. Do you view your clothing as a way to cover your body comfortably, or are clothes also a form of self-expression or creativity? Do your clothes reflect your authentic tastes or do they change with each blip in fashion trends? Do you have a lot of clothes you don't wear? Why? Is it important to you to have a large closet crammed with clothes? What does that mean to you?

> *The collector walks with blinders on; he sees nothing but the prize. In fact, the acquisitive instinct is incompatible with true appreciation of beauty.*
>
> Anne Morrow Lindbergh

We acquire things to serve many different purposes—practical functions, respect, excitement, variety, beauty, and entertainment, to name a few. The objective is to be conscious of why we purchase what we purchase so we can evaluate whether we are getting the value we seek from our possessions. As we simplify our lives and experience more fulfillment from experiences than things, we naturally become more discriminating about what possessions we bring into our lives.

I've noticed that European women seem to have less variety in their wardrobes than American women. To my eye, European women tend to wear fewer colors, enabling them to mix and match more easily. Overall, their clothes seem to be of a higher quality than much of what you see in America. A wardrobe of fewer, more beautiful, more durable pieces requires less investment of time, energy, and money while providing greater comfort and visual pleasure. What a concept!

Sometimes we keep things long after they have served any purpose. For example, my husband and I carted his old college textbooks (terribly outdated and never looked at) from house to house for years before he was able to let go of them. It's helpful to ask ourselves what our possessions say about us. Do we keep unused, unvalued books because it makes us look smart to have full bookshelves in every room? Do we bring home all sorts of momentos from our travels because they bring back fond memories, or because we can impress our guests with how well travelled we are? As you complete the lesson assignments below, ask yourself what significance you place on your possessions. You will likely find it to be an enlightening exercise.

THE IMPACT OF OUR CONSUMPTION PRACTICES

One man's enough is another's privation.

Jessamyn West

The manufacture and ultimate disposal of material goods depletes natural resources. As noted in Lesson 1, Americans consume far more resources per capita than many other countries. In Lesson 12, we will explore the issues related to environmental sustainability in more depth. For now, as we examine our relationship to material goods, we should keep in mind that our choices have an impact beyond our individual lives.

Natural resources are also used to transport goods to the consumer. For that reason, many people buy locally-produced products when possible, even if the cost is higher. In addition to conserving resources, buying locally also supports the economic well-being of the community.

Consumption practices also affect the issues of globalization and social equity. For example, does the purchase of goods produced by workers in so-called sweatshops in less industrialized countries further the oppression of these workers? Some people choose not to purchase such goods for this reason. Similarly, you can support social equity by buying goods that are produced with certain standards of fairness and equity for workers, as in the case of fair trade coffee. Fair trade coffee certification programs seek to establish a fair and equitable partnership between North American coffee consumers and coffee farmers in Asia, Africa, Latin America, and the Caribbean by requiring minimum levels of compensation to be paid to coffee farmers.

The full global impact of our consumption practices is a complex subject and beyond the scope of this book. If you are interested in exploring these issues in more depth, you should read

Alan Durning's books (see Recommended Resources at the end of this lesson) or some of the books recommended in Lesson 12.

REDUCING CONSUMPTION

Reducing consumption of material goods has at least three benefits: it preserves the earth's resources, it facilitates living on less income (enabling fewer work hours), and it saves enormous amounts of personal time and energy required for the acquisition, storage, maintenance, insurance, and eventual disposal of goods.

As individuals and families, we can choose to consume less. But it can be difficult to buck the status quo of mainstream culture. And even if we do consume less, our individual contribution to the earth's resources may be overshadowed by the millions of people who consume excessively.

He who buys what he does not want ends in wanting what he cannot buy.

Mrs. Alec-Tweedie

As a society, what can we do to motivate people to consume less? Our purpose here is to brainstorm—to explore incentives to consume less in ways acceptable to the majority. I will present a few ideas to get you started. Your job is to ponder it further and come up with your own ideas.

Let's start with financial incentives. In 2002, Ireland imposed a 15-cent levy on each plastic bag given out by retailers, resulting in a 90 percent decline in requests for plastic bags. It's fairly easy to use cloth bags or used plastic bags for shopping. All we need is a little incentive. Ireland's plastic bag taxes netted over three million dollars in just a few months. Those taxes will be used by the Irish government to protect the environment.[2]

North Americans could do the same thing, not only with plastic bags but with other products and packaging materials that contribute to the degradation of the environment. The proceeds could be used for programs that alleviate the environmental damage caused by our consumption. Rather than view these taxes as a penalty, they should be considered a *pay as you go* contribution. We take from the earth. Is it not reasonable to make a contribution for the benefit of the earth?

Similarly, we could shift our tax structure to rely less on income taxes and more on sales or use taxes levied on non-essential items. This is a complex issue and has the risk of imposing a proportionately greater tax burden on people with lower incomes, which is clearly not a desired outcome.

But let's play with this idea a little further. The challenge of reaching a consensus on the meaning of *non-essential items* is substantial. For example, how many television sets are *essential* for a household? Would we exempt taxes for the first television, but impose taxes for the second and subsequent televisions? And while there are luxury taxes on certain big-ticket items, we don't impose additional taxes on a person who buys 100 pairs of shoes.

I like to go to Marshall Field's in Chicago just to see how many things there are in the world that I do not want.

Mother M. Madeleva

There are, of course, political issues to consider. Many argue for less governmental involvement in our personal lives. In the United States, we place a high value on personal freedom. Free enterprise is part of the mission statement of this country. We take pride in what we have accomplished as a result of these principles. If someone wants to buy 100 pairs of shoes, she should be able to, we say. However, it could be argued that this essential freedom is not diminished by an earth tax. Such a tax is merely an equitable contribution to offset the damage to the earth from our consumption practices.

There is also the question of how feasible—from a practical and economical viewpoint—it would be to enforce such laws. Businesses would scream in protest at any incentive that would lead Americans to spend less. In our country, we assume perennial economic growth is vital and desirable, but we fail to consider the consequences of this way of life, both to the earth and to the quality of our lives.

A less controversial financial incentive would be to further increase tax benefits for retirement saving programs. Today, people participate in forced savings programs by authorizing paycheck deductions for their 401k plans or by contributing to KEOGH and IRA plans. In theory, these savings plans result in less money to spend on material goods. However, some do not spend less; they simply increase their credit card debt. Others take advantage of greater retirement savings tax benefits without increasing their debt. Additional retirement savings incentives would provide some incentive to consume less.

Undoubtedly, there are other ways to encourage people to consume less. For example, to the extent excessive spending is a result of too much stress from work or insufficient family and community involvement, addressing those needs directly will have a positive effect on consumption levels. Educating people about the harmful effects of excessive consumption on the environment will lead some people to consume less.

In group discussions on this subject, there is usually one person who asks, "What about the economy? If everyone consumed less, our economy would collapse and millions of people would be unemployed." There is no question that if North Americans immediately reduced its consumption levels by half, for example, we would have a serious employment problem in this country. This prospect is highly unlikely because human beings simply don't change that quickly. Even if there were widespread interest in reducing consumption, it would take some years to implement a noticeable change. Economic markets for housing, labor, and goods would adjust gradually to reflect a new economy.

Too much good fortune can make you smug and unaware. Happiness should be like an oasis, the greener for the desert that surrounds it.

Rachel Field

We worship economic growth in the United States. After the tragic events of September 11, 2001, our president told us that it was our patriotic duty to go out and spend to avoid any disruption of economic growth. But for what purpose are we growing? In Lesson 1, we considered the fact that even though our per capita spending has more than tripled in the last 50 years, we are no happier or more fulfilled. The United States was founded for the purpose of offering its citizens "life, liberty, and the pursuit of happiness." When did we replace those ideals with working to exhaustion and spending excessively?

CONCLUSION

People who live simply consciously choose their material possessions rather than obey cultural mandates to always buy more. Generally they discover (often quite unexpectedly) they need and want far fewer possessions than the mainstream. This is how it works: when you live simply, you slow down. When you slow down, you become more conscious of everything in your life, including your possessions. This awareness engenders a deeper understanding of what our lives are about. Often we develop gratitude and a greater sensitivity to the material waste in our culture. We simply don't want things we don't value in our space. "Get it out of here!" we scream. With fewer possessions, it's much easier to develop a genuine love and appreciation for the things you keep in your life. The goal, then, is to take what you need or cherish and to honor the life energy and natural resources that went into producing your possessions by taking good care of them. We let go of everything else.

As for things, how they do accumulate, how often I wish to exclaim, "Oh, don't *give me that!*"

Susan Hale

LESSON ASSIGNMENTS

FROM YOUR PERSONAL VIEWPOINT . . .

1. List three to five things that you own and genuinely cherish. If you are a member of a study group, choose one of those items to discuss with the group. Share why you cherish it.
2. List three to five things that you own and feel burdened by. If you are a member of a study a group, choose one of those items to discuss with the group. Share the nature of the burden you feel.
3. Think of one thing you bought and never used. Then tell the story of how and why you bought it, whether you are ready to let it go, and how you might accomplish this. If you are a member of a group, bring this item for show and tell.
4. Think of an item you own that required a lot more time and energy to acquire, maintain or dispose of than you expected. Describe what time you spent on that item.
5. If you had 10 minutes to evacuate your home due to an impending fire or other disaster, what would you take? What would you miss of the things you left behind (assuming you had sufficient insurance money to replace your basic necessities)?
6. Do you feel that your self-esteem is affected by what you own or possess? If so, what items enhance your self-esteem? Do you feel that others think more highly of you based on what you own? If so, what are some examples?
7. Do you feel that your stuff is an expression of who you are, meaning is it a form of creative self-expression? If so, describe which items fit into that category for you?

8. Do you enjoy shopping? What does it do for you? Does it serve other needs unrelated to the goods you purchase?
9. Do you have certain consumption patterns that you would like to reduce? What are some possible approaches to accomplishing this?

LOOKING AT THE BIGGER PICTURE . . .

10. Do you feel that society pressures us into consuming more than we want or need? Where does this pressure come from? How have you felt this pressure in your own life?
11. Identify one to three advertisements in the print media that promise intangible benefits (such as happiness, security, or sex appeal) from the product or service being sold. Discuss the truth or falsity of such promises. If you are a member of a group, bring a copy of the ad to share with others.
12. What types of pressures do children feel relating to the consumption of material goods? What are some creative ways to relieve this pressure?
13. Try to come up with one or more public policies that would encourage people to consume less. Don't worry about the practicalities at this point. Think big.
14. Is there something that can be done (or is being done) in your community to support the choice to consume less?

Advertisement . . . has brought our disregard for truth into the open without even a figleaf to cover it.

Freya Stark

LIFEWORK ASSIGNMENTS

1. Go through your possessions and weed out anything you haven't used in a year, except for sentimental items such as photographs. Get rid of whatever you don't need or cherish it. If you're unsure, pack it away and mark a date on the box for one year later. If, within that year, you have no occasion to unpack that box, sell or give away the contents. If this assignment feels overwhelming, try one drawer or closet a week. Even if it takes a full year to complete the process, you are likely to experience a feeling of liberation and lightness that will carry over to other areas of your life.

2. Take a physical inventory of the goods in your house. Start with one area—your wardrobe is a good choice. The kitchen is another. Write down the total number of items within each category. For example, if you are a woman who selects clothes, you might have a list like this (but do not place any significance on the numbers used):

Long pants	8	Robes	1
Skirts	6	Pajamas/nightgowns	3
Dresses	5	Belts	5
Short pants/shorts	4	Scarves	7
Tops/shirts/blouses	15	Hats	5
Sweaters	10	Gloves (pairs)	3
Bras	5	Coats/jackets	10
Panties	10	Shoes/sandals (pairs)	15
Socks/nylon stockings (pairs)	10	Boots (pairs)	2
Swimsuits	2	Sport-specific shoes & boots	4

My mother insisted that I had to try things on to make sure they were becoming. Becoming what, I always asked.

Edith Konecky

Feel free to customize the categories to conform to your wardrobe. The point is to account for every item of clothing you own (wherever it may be hidden in your home or garage) in one category or another. Once you complete this list, just let it sit. Try not to judge yourself. Just let it sit for awhile.

After you have lived with your inventory list for a few weeks, take another look at it. Ask yourself whether you need or cherish all the items in each category. For example, if you have 20 sweaters but only wear four or five of them regularly, perhaps there are several or many that fail the need/cherish test. When you are ready to let them go, do so. The value of this exercise is based on the fact that awareness by itself will often lead us to make positive changes in our lives. Don't force yourself. Go at your own pace. Remember, simplicity is not about deprivation.

3. Consider adopting a *purchase manifesto*, a checklist of the points you want to consider before purchasing material goods. You can carry this in your wallet for easy reference. Here is the one used by John Stott of Madison, Wisconsin:

- Aesthetic/appeal
- Versatility/functionality
- Earth friendly
- Well made/repairable—Is there a warranty?
- Value—would a used version be just as good or better?
- Consider substitutions
- Do I really need this?

4. If you are a parent with children at home, talk to your kids about their clothes and toys. Ask them which items they need or really love. If there are clothes or toys they never use, suggest they give them to another child who could use them. Children seem to feel better about letting go of stuff when they can give it to another child. Another potentially rewarding experience for your children is a holiday giving program. Some charitable and community groups organize programs in which one family can sponsor another family for a holiday. Often the sponsoring family will purchase a holiday tree, gifts, and food for a less-advantaged (materially, that is) family and deliver them in person. If there is an opportunity for your children to participate in such a program, it will give them a new perspective on possessions and help them develop a deeper gratitude for what they have.
5. If you are inclined toward activism, consider what may be done in your community to encourage people to consume less. For example, you might try to get your local newspaper to write a story about people living simply in your community. Or you might start a simplicity study group. Be creative.

I base most of my fashion taste on what doesn't itch.

Gilda Radner

ANNUAL CHECK-UP

1. Once a year, go through your stuff and weed out anything that is no longer valuable to you.
2. Review the lifework assignments to see if you would like to take on one or more of these projects.

RECOMMENDED RESOURCES

Books

30 Days to a Simpler Life by Connie Cox and Cris Evatt (New York: The Penguin Group, 1998). Practical guide for organizing living spaces, including offices, wardrobes, photos, books, and magazines. Travel, financial planning, and leisure are also covered.

Clutter Control: Putting Your Home on a Diet by Jeff Campbell (New York: Dell Publishing, 1992). Discusses both the physical and psychological aspects of managing material possessions. Suggests ways to minimize the negative impact of too much clutter.

Clutter's Last Stand: It's Time to De-Junk Your Life by Don Aslett (Cincinnati: Writer's Digest Books, 1984). Discusses the stuff in our lives—why we buy it, why we hoard it well beyond its pleasurable or useful life, and how to let go of it. Also explores mental clutter, such as money (tracking it, investing it, and managing it), people, and activities that complicate your life.

The High Price of Materialism by Tim Kasser (Boston: MIT Press, 2002). Psychology professor offers a scientific explanation of how our contemporary culture of consumerism and materialism affects our everyday happiness and psychological health, including anxiety, depression, low self-esteem, and problems with intimacy.

How Much is Enough?: The Consumer Society and the Future of the Earth by Alan Durning (New York: W.W. Norton, 1992). Provides a comprehensive overview of the consumer society—how we got to where we are, the damage done to the earth by the consumer class, and the striking lack of fulfillment resulting from the consumer way of life. The author argues that true fulfillment comes from the nonmaterial aspects of life, such as relationships, work, and leisure.

The Overspent American: Why We Want What We Don't Need by Juliet B. Schor (New York: HarperCollins, 1999). Explores America's relationship with its spending patterns—why and how we spend and consume—focusing on the psychological motivations for excessive spending, including the desire to gain status relative to others. Profiles people who have downshifted as an alternative to a life heavily based on consumerism.

Stuff: The Secret Lives of Everyday Things by John C. Ryan and Alan Durning (Seattle: Northwest Environment Watch, 1997). Enlightening read that traces the environmental history and impact of goods consumed by the average American.

MISCELLANEOUS

The Center for a New American Dream [www.newdream.org] is a not-for-profit membership-based organization that helps individuals and institutions reduce and shift consumption to enhance quality of life and protect the environment.

Adbusters Magazine [www.adbusters.org/magazine] is published by the Adbusters Media Foundation, a Vancouver, B.C. based non-profit organization committed to forcing a major paradigm shift in North America and throughout the world towards a more ecologically sustainable environment. In addition to its magazine, the group sponsors anti-commercial campaigns, such as *Buy Nothing Day* (the day after Thanksgiving), and operates *Powershift*, an advocacy advertising agency.

NOTE: *Additions and updates to these resources can be found on The Simplicity Resource Guide at www.gallagherpress.com/pierce.*

LESSON 3

MAKING FRIENDS WITH MONEY

HOW MUCH IS ENOUGH?

Ah, money . . . we love it, we hate it, we never have enough. Have you ever heard anyone complain of having too much money? Ironically, as Jessie O'Neill explains in her book, *The Golden Ghetto*, wealthy people struggle to be happy as much or more than the rest of us. Current academic research studies support this contention.[1] Even though we've heard a thousand times that money doesn't buy happiness, we don't quite believe it.

My husband buys an occasional lottery ticket and I pray he doesn't win. So far, my prayers have been answered. Excessive amounts of money would give me a new part-time job of investing the proceeds and selecting donation recipients among hundreds of worthy candidates. I already have a job I love—writing and speaking about voluntary simplicity. I don't need another one. I am also concerned that unlimited funds would tempt me to embrace a life of luxury that would detract from the peace and fulfillment I now have in my life. Naturally, many friends have offered to relieve me of this burden should my husband's luck turn.

Often I hear people say that simplicity is for those who can afford to live simply, meaning that it's easy to live simply when you have plenty of money. I doubt it. If you have more money than you can possibly use, how easy would it be to choose nonmaterial rewards over the immediate pleasures of material comforts? The reverse is also true. It is impossible to live simply if you have inadequate means to meet your basic physical needs. No one should confuse voluntary simplicity with involuntary poverty.

So, once again, we come back to our recurring question, "How much is enough?" Surveys indicate that *enough* is always slightly beyond our current means, that we never in fact reach the state of having enough money.[2] This inquiry—how much is enough—would appear to be fairly straightforward. We can simply total our current expenses, add an estimated amount for those things we want and don't yet have, and press the enter key. Right?

In fact, there's more to it. Somehow we need to differentiate in our minds our authentic desires for money from the pressures of societal expectations. For example, consider how much we associate earning potential with a person's career status and inherent value to society. Would lawyers and doctors be treated with the same respect if they earned a teacher's salary and teachers earned the big bucks? My guess is that our respect would go to whoever earns the most money.

Traditionally, women are taught to seek mates who are good providers. In industrialized countries, we associate being a good provider with earning a high income even though, ironically, the very act of earning a high income often prevents a man from providing his family what they need most—his being present and engaged in a life outside his work.

Too many people spend money they haven't earned, to buy things they don't want, to impress people they don't like.

Will Rogers

EXPLORING YOUR RELATIONSHIP WITH MONEY

The objective is not to love or hate money but rather to make peace with money. If you see money as your enemy—if you engage in a life-long battle with money—it will cause you nothing but grief. We can relate to money in different ways. We can feel victimized if we don't have enough money or guilty if we have more than others and don't share enough. We can deny its role in our lives, spending beyond our means. We can be addicted to making money or hoarding money. We can equate our net worth with our self-worth. Or we can view money as a welcoming, useful resource, believing that its purpose is to help us meet our basic needs and to provide a means to experience life fully. Rather than viewing money as the source of ultimate happiness, or disparaging it as an expression of greed, we can recognize money for what it is—a form of exchange, an efficient mechanism to swap goods and services.

In our quest to make money our friend, we must first become acquainted with it. We start by determining what money comes in and goes out of our lives. Vicki Robin and the late Joe Dominguez wrote an excellent book about money. In *Your Money or Your Life*, the authors describe money as a form of life energy—the energy it takes to earn and manage the money you spend. They suggest you first determine how much life energy is expended for those things requiring money (like housing, transportation, food, and clothing), and then evaluate whether you are getting good value for your life energy. For example, if you dine out three or four nights a week and you determine that this practice requires you to work one full day a week, you can then ask yourself whether it is worth it or not. Each person and family must decide how much is enough on a material scale. We will use the principles of *Your Money or Your Life* in this lesson to help determine that question for ourselves.

FINANCIAL INDEPENDENCE

The authors of *Your Money or Your Life* contend that financial independence is a worthy goal. Some people misunderstand this concept. They assume that the objective is to get to a point where you no longer need to work. To the contrary, purposeful work is a rewarding part of human life, whether you're financially independent or not. The beauty of financial independence is that you can do exactly the work you choose (whether paid or not) without concerns for the basic necessities of life. That is not to say, however, that you can't live a fulfilling, rewarding life without financial independence. You most certainly can. It's just that you have more freedom in your work choices if you don't need to concern yourself with paying the bills.

We both deplore extravagance. He deplores mine, and I deplore his.

Jane Goodsell

CAN YOU AFFORD TO WORK?

Do you know how much money you earn? Of course, you do. But let's take another look. Let's calculate your true hourly compensation. I will explain the process and then you can do this for yourself as outlined in the lesson assignments below. First, determine the gross amount you earn on a weekly basis. If you are paid monthly, divide that figure by 4.3, the average number of weeks in a month. The next step is to deduct the costs you incur for the pleasure of working. There are income taxes, of course, as well as other expenses that pertain exclusively to your work. For example, there are costs to commute to your job, which may include the expense of an additional car in your household. If your family includes two income earners, ask yourself if you could manage with one less car if only one of you worked. If the answer is yes, the total costs of the second car (amortized on a weekly basis) should be deducted from your weekly compensation.

Other potential work-related expenses include day care costs, the incremental cost to buy lunch out versus eating at home, costs for a work wardrobe, and the incremental cost to buy prepared food or to dine in restaurants because you are too tired to cook. There is also the cost for household and gardening help that you might otherwise do yourself if you were not working.

The one with the primary responsibility to the individual's future is that individual.

Dorcas Hardy

Let's consider a hypothetical example. Susan works full-time for an annual income of $50,000 or $1,000 per week, assuming two weeks of vacation. At first glance, it would appear that she earns $25 per hour. However, as discussed above, we need to deduct her work-related expenses (amortized on a weekly basis), such as income taxes ($250), child care ($150), commuting costs ($120), work clothes ($30), and the incremental costs for lunches, prepared food, and dinners out ($50). This results in a more accurate weekly compensation of $400.

To determine Susan's true hourly rate, we should divide $400 by the number of hours she works each week. Susan's boss expects her to work 40 hours, but, for our purposes, we need to add in the hours spent on job-related activities, such as commuting to work, dressing for work (beyond what it would take to throw on jeans and a sweatshirt for a non-work day), and the time to drop off and pick up her children from day care. What appears on the surface to be a 40-hour a week job could easily take 52 hours of Susan's time. In this example, we divide $400 by 52 hours to determine that Susan earns $7.69 an hour, a far cry from the $25 per hour job offer she thought she had accepted. Susan would probably be shocked to know her true hourly rate.

Based on the guidelines in *Your Money or Your Life*, Susan would then use her life energy rate of $7.69 per hour to determine how much life energy is required for various expenditures. For example, if Susan buys a dress for $100, she needs to work 13 hours (100 divided by $7.69) to pay for that dress. Only Susan can decide if the dress is worth 13 hours of her labor.

One thing we learn as we proceed down the path of simplicity is that money isn't everything, nor is it even the most important thing in life (assuming that basic physical needs are met). Perhaps Susan loves her work and has enough money to meet her needs, possibly with the contribution of a spouse's income. On the other hand, Susan may prefer to stay home with her children or work part-time to pursue other interests, but she has always viewed these options as economically unfeasible. Knowing her true hourly compensation is essential for Susan to accurately compare the monetary value of her various options.

Understanding the often-overlooked costs of working in a traditional job leads some people to favor work that can be done at home or at a job that is closer to home, saving time and money on a long commute while potentially earning greater hourly compensation. It's not at all uncommon for a valued employee to quit his job but then continue to work from home as an independent contractor, working fewer hours and earning more money.

If you do nothing unexpected, nothing unexpected happens.

Fay Weldon

When you compare compensation levels of various work opportunities, you also need to factor in the value of any benefits, primarily health insurance (if you live in the United States). For this purpose, you can estimate the value of health insurance provided by your employer by obtaining a quote for what it would cost you to purchase such insurance independently as an individual or family.

In the lesson assignments below, you will be asked to calculate your true hourly compensation—assuming you work for money—using the Hourly Compensation Worksheet on page 197. (Even if you work as a volunteer, you can still calculate the expense side of your work.) The point of this exercise is to get an accurate reading of the net amount you receive from your work. Only then can you decide whether it is worth staying with your current job or making a change.

HEALTH INSURANCE

I once heard a person say, "My job is killing me, but I can't quit because of health insurance." Hmmm . . . what's wrong with *that* picture? If you live in Canada, Europe, or another country that provides health insurance to its citizenry, feel free to skip this section, unless you would like to experience a moment of gratitude.

The path to simplicity is littered with complexities.

Susan Ohanian

There is no question that health insurance costs in the United States have skyrocketed during the last 10 years. Recently, the health insurance premium for my husband and me (both healthy fifty-somethings) increased to over $700 per month. I'm sure we could get better rates if we didn't insist on living in one of the most expensive states (California) in the country. But here is the bottom line about health insurance: if you are healthy, you can obtain health insurance as an individual or family. You do not need to stay in your job for health insurance purposes. Yes, it will cost you more to purchase an individual policy. But that cost is no different than other costs of living, such as housing, transportation, food, and clothing. It is just one piece of the overall mosaic of financial responsibility—living within your means, spending less than you earn. So, hypothetically, if you quit a job to work at home, your commute cost savings may offset the health insurance premium you would pay for an individual policy.

When I conducted *The Pierce Simplicity Study*, I talked to a number of people who choose to live without health insurance. Typically, these people maintain excellent health practices and believe their risk of getting a serious illness or injury is low. However, drunk drivers and other agents of accidents do not discriminate based on the health status of their victims. And consider this: the vast majority of women diagnosed with breast cancer have no discernable risk factors for the disease.[3]

Some people reasonably assume they will get medical care for serious ailments even if they don't have insurance. In fact, U.S. federal and various state programs provide some health care for those who don't have insurance and cannot afford to pay for the care. Additionally, medical providers will sometimes absorb health care costs for the truly indigent, ensuring their profitability by charging higher rates for those who can afford to pay. But unless you are truly poor, it's unlikely that you'll get a free ride on medical care. In essence, health insurance does not protect your health as much as it protects your savings, the equity in your home, and your future wages. Ultimately, the decision to go without health insurance is a matter of risk tolerance.

YOUR FINANCIAL OVERVIEW

We have looked at work compensation and health insurance issues in a new light. Now it's time to get a more complete overview of your finances. The most essential element of simplicity is to live consciously and deliberately. Awareness of how we spend our money—our life energy—is critical.

In the lesson assignments below, you will be asked to complete the Money Worksheet. If you already keep track of the money in your life, you can use your own financial reports instead. Writing down what money comes in and what goes out is like writing down what you eat every day. If you really know everything you eat, you are inclined to make adjustments. Similarly, the simple knowledge of what you are doing with your money will likely lead you to cut back on expenditures that don't offer good value for your life energy.

Debt is the sort of Bedfellow who is forever pulling all the Covers his way.

Minna Thomas Antrim

LOOKING AT THE NOT-SO-PRETTY BIG PICTURE

Consider these facts for the United States. More people file for personal bankruptcy than graduate from college each year.[4] It's not surprising that we spend more money on clothes than on higher education.[5] Consumer credit debt more than doubled between 1990 ($789 billion) and 2001 ($1,668 billion).[6] Meanwhile our national savings rate has decreased from about 10 percent of disposable income in 1980 to a rate of zero in 2000.[7]

We work and spend while suffering a poverty of spirit. What can we do as a society to encourage people to live with financial integrity and responsibility? Education is, I believe, our most hopeful tool. Here are just a few ideas in that direction:

- Require all high school students to complete a semester course on money (covering management, investment, mortgages, credit cards, bank statements, and the like) in order to graduate. Such a course would counterbalance the influx of unsolicited credit cards distributed to college students, who, experiencing their first taste of financial power, sometimes let their spending get out of control.

- Require any person seeking relief in bankruptcy courts to complete a similar course on money management.

Perhaps, we could enact laws that would ensure that credit card accounts were issued only to those people who have reached a certain level of maturity. For example, if we restricted credit card companies from issuing cards to minors unless a parent or guardian co-signed for the debt in advance, chances are we would have far fewer credit card abuses.

In this lesson, you will have the opportunity to devise your own creative solutions to the problem of systemic overspending in North America.

Until you make peace with who you are, you'll never be content with what you have.

Doris Mortman

CONCLUSION

In the United States, the subject of money often dominates our thoughts. We can obsess with getting it, losing it, or not having enough. Too often, we associate money with self-worth. If we fear we will never have enough money, it can be a self-fulfilling prophecy. If, on the other hand, we assume we will have enough, it is likely we will take steps to make that happen.

The key to your relationship with money is to make peace with it. Treat it as you would a friend—with trust, respect, and openness.

LESSON ASSIGNMENTS

FROM YOUR PERSONAL VIEWPOINT . . .

1. If you work for money, prepare the Hourly Compensation Worksheet on page 197. If you work as a volunteer, prepare the expenses portion of the Worksheet. If you are a student and receive funding from loans or parents, include those sources of income as compensation.
2. Complete the Money Worksheet on page 198. As discussed above, until you know where your money goes, you cannot make conscious choices on how to spend it. (Note: don't feel any obligation to share your financial information with others in the group, but do share whatever you care to about what you learned from doing the exercise).

3. How much debt do you and your family owe, aside from a mortgage on the home you live in? How do you feel about this level of debt? If you believe it is too high, what can you do to reduce your debt (see the Lifework Assignments below)?
4. What lessons about money were you taught as a child growing up? As a young adult, what beliefs did you (or do you) hold about money?
5. Think about the relationship between money and happiness. Do you view money as the key to your happiness? How much more money, if any, would you need to be truly happy? Could there ever be such a thing as too much money in your life?
6. Are you at peace with your financial decisions? Or do you struggle with the money issues in your life, possibly by spending unconsciously, or refusing to look at how you spend your money, or feeling a victim of insufficient monetary resources?
7. What does money say (or not say) about who you are as a person?
8. How important is financial security to you? What does it mean to you? Having enough for the next six months' or one year's expenses? Or having enough so that you never need to work again?
9. Is there anything in your relationship with money that you want to change? Any changes in patterns of spending or earning income? What are some ways you can accomplish those changes?

LOOKING AT THE BIGGER PICTURE . . .

10. What does your culture teach you about money? Do you think society values people according to their income? Is money valued primarily for what you can get with it or does it have an inherent value apart from this function?
11. What can we do as a society to encourage people to live with financial integrity and responsibility? Can you think of any social or public policies that would further this goal? Be as specific as possible.

It is not easy to find happiness in ourselves, and it is not possible to find it elsewhere.

Agnes Repplier

Abundance is, in large part, an attitude.

Sue Patton Thoele

LIFEWORK ASSIGNMENTS

1. Consider keeping track of the money that comes in and goes out of your life on a regular basis. Ideally, you should review your finances once a month. Many people use Quicken® or similar software for this purpose. You can also just make a written list of your income and expenditures each month. This exercise is valuable because it helps you pay attention to your spending habits. As with most things in life, awareness is half the battle.
2. If you or your family spend more than you earn on a regular basis, identify one or more ways you can reduce your expenses or increase your income, and then set goals to accomplish these objectives. Start gradually and work in small steps.
3. If you have problems meeting the minimum payments on your debts, come up with a plan to reduce your debt. The Consumer Credit Counseling Service (CCCS), an organization with over 1,300 community-based offices, provides free or low cost services to people who have lost control of their debt.

ANNUAL CHECK-UP

1. Once a year, it is advisable to do a more thorough review of your finances. Hopefully you have been monitoring your income and expenses throughout the year. If not, complete the Money Worksheet to get a current view of your finances. Have you noticed any positive or negative trends in your financial picture?
2. This is also a good time to review your investment and retirement savings strategies to see if you want to make any changes.
3. Now that you have a current view of your finances, you may want to draft a budget or financial plan for the coming year.

RECOMMENDED RESOURCES

Books

Cheap Talk with the Frugal Friends: Over 600 Tips, Tricks, and Creative Ideas for Saving Money by Angie Zalewski and Deana Ricks (Lancaster, PA: Starburst Publishers, 2001). Includes money-saving tips in areas of groceries, recycling, garage sales, sports, children, pets, travel, entertaining, gifts, clothes and beauty, automobiles, and more.

The Complete Tightwad Gazette: Promoting Thrift as a Viable Alternative Lifestyle by Amy Dacyczn (New York: Random House, 1999). Consolidates material from the author's former newsletter and books. Includes detailed, practical, and thoroughly researched ideas for ways to live frugally.

Getting a Life: Strategies for Simple Living Based on the Revolutionary Program for Financial Freedom from Your Money or Your Life by Jacqueline Blix and David Heitmiller (New York: Viking Penguin, Revised 1999). Features detailed life stories of people who have used the nine-step program in *Your Money or Your Life* to live with greater financial intelligence, financial integrity, and in some cases, financial independence.

The Golden Ghetto: The Psychology of Affluence by Jessie O'Neill (Milwaukee, WI: The Affluenza Project, 1997). Psychotherapist who grew up with wealth explores the challenging and potentially dysfunctional aspects of living with wealth. Provides an inside view of the myths that more is better and that wealth brings happiness.

How to Survive Without a Salary: Learning to Live the Conserver Lifestyle by Charles Long (Toronto: Warwick Publishing, Revised 1996). Discusses the *conserver* lifestyle—reducing expenses, saving, and earning casual income. Promotes value of earning casual income rather than work in a salaried job.

Miserly Moms: Living on One Income in a Two-Income Economy by Jonni McCoy (Minneapolis, MN: Bethany House, 3rd edition, 2001). Practical guide by stay-at-home mom on how to reduce family living expenses. Emphasis on food costs, planning, and recipes.

Shattering the Two-Income Myth: Daily Secrets for Living Well on One Income by Andy Dappen (Mountlake Terrace, WA: Brier Books, 1997). Thoughtful summary of why and how we evolved into a two-income society, as well as practical advice on how to live on one income.

Your Money or Your Life: Transforming Your Relationship with Money and Achieving Financial Independence by Joe Dominguez and Vicki Robin (New York: Penguin Books, Revised 1999). Bestselling classic of the voluntary simplicity movement. Presents a nine-step program to reach financial independence. Discusses how to live a high quality of life with fewer materialistic trappings and help save the earth at the same time.

MISCELLANEOUS

Consumer Credit Counseling Service (CCCS) [www.nfcc.org] is a nonprofit organization that offers educational and planning services to people who are struggling with debt. Member agencies are credited by the National Foundation for Credit Counseling. You can obtain confidential counseling online, via the telephone, or from one of its 1,300 community-based offices.

The Dollar Stretcher [www.dollarstretcher.com] features a free, weekly email newsletter packed with useful articles on living simply and frugally. The web site includes archives of past articles.

Frugal Fun [www.frugalfun.com] offers articles to help you save you money and enjoy more of life at less cost. Also includes articles on building a business on a budget.

The Frugal Life [www.thefrugallife.com] offers a free email newsletter and a community forum in which people can ask questions and share their experiences of living simply and frugally.

A *Frugal, Simple Life* [hometown.aol.com/DSimple/index.html] is a website maintained by Deborah Taylor-Hough, author of *Frozen Assets* and A *Simple Choice*. In addition to many frugal living tips on the web site, Deborah publishes a free email newsletter, *Simple Times*.

NOTE: *Additions and updates to these resources can be found on The Simplicity Resource Guide at www.gallagherpress.com/pierce.*

LESSON 4

Home is Where the Heart Lives

HOME SWEET HOME — COZY RETREAT OR PART-TIME JOB?

There are few things more precious to us than our homes. Even the most thrilling vacation does not diminish the sweetness of coming home. Unless you are a hopeless workaholic, you will spend more time in your home than anywhere else. For most of us, our homes—size, aesthetics, floor plan, and location—greatly affect our sense of well-being.

The average home size in the United States has more than doubled in the last 50 years, from 1,100 square feet in the 1950's to 2,300 square feet today,[1] which is more than twice the average home sizes in most of Europe.[2] With the current median size of 2,100 square feet, it is a fair bet that there are as many 3,000 square-foot homes as 1,000 square-foot homes. Why do we need or want larger homes? The average household size has decreased during the same 50-year period.[3] Extra space may be needed for large families or at-home workers, but many people who live in large homes occupy just a few rooms, leaving the remaining space vacant except for infrequent social gatherings or out-of-town guests.

Owning your own home was once the American dream. Now, trading up to a larger, more prestigious home is the desired goal. We have evolved from wanting an aesthetically pleasing, comfortable abode to viewing our homes as status symbols or a reflection of personal success. The larger and grander our home, the more important we think we are.

Again, we come back to the question, "How much is enough?" How many rooms do we need? How large should they be to provide optimum comfort without adding unnecessary maintenance and furniture expenses? In addition to kitchens and family rooms—where we really live—we often tell ourselves we need a formal living room and a separate dining room, even though we rarely spend time in those rooms. We *need* these formal rooms to entertain friends and business associates, even though more often than not, our guests prefer to hang out in the kitchen or family room when they visit. We also *need* these formal rooms to boost resale value, so we can sell our house to another family who will not use these rooms any more than we did.

Television has become a pervasive part of our lives, and each family member has his own favorite shows. Thus, we *need* separate spaces for TV viewing. Before television, it was common for families to gather in the living room after supper for shared activities—reading, school homework, playing board games, or engaging in various hobbies. Today, everyone scatters to separate rooms where they indulge in their separate pastimes.

Additional reasonably sized rooms may be very appropriate if one or more family members are engaged in a home-based business or active hobbies. A room designated for an active hobby does not include a room whose main purpose is to house a pool table used two or three times a year when Uncle Ted visits.

That's all your house is: a place to keep your stuff. If you didn't have so much stuff, you wouldn't need a house. You could just walk around all the time. A house is just a pile of stuff with a cover on it.

George Carlin

Ideally, someone would use each room in your house every day for one purpose or another. Some rooms can easily be used for dual purposes. For example, my home office doubles as a guest bedroom the few times a year we have overnight guests. We simply move my desk out of the way and pull out the queen-sized futon bed. (This arrangement has the added benefit of discouraging me from working when we have guests.)

An extra room may also be appropriate if used frequently though not daily. For example, my brother and sister-in-law exude hospitality and consequently have a constant flow of overnight guests. One often needs to make a reservation for the *pink room*, a room reserved exclusively for guests. Some people with large homes host frequent community gatherings, making excellent use of their extra space. There are no rigid rules about how much space is appropriate, except that you should use what you have on a regular basis. The bottom line about space: use it or lose it—move to smaller quarters.

There are alternatives to buying and maintaining homes that will accommodate guests. For those occasional family reunions or large parties, it can be cost effective to rent other space, such as a small bed and breakfast inn or a banquet hall. Or you could offer to pay for your guest's hotel bill instead of buying a home large enough to accommodate infrequent visitors.

In *The Not So Big House*, architect Sarah Susanka proposes

that homes should be beautiful and cozy with rooms to scale in proportion to the human form. With the growth of so-called trophy homes that look more like museums than places of comfort and retreat, we have lost some of the nurturing value of our homes. Remember when you were a kid and loved to crawl into cardboard forts, attic spaces, and other makeshift cubbyholes? We humans desire spaces that provide a sheltering feeling of comfort and protection. Unfortunately, in North America we gravitate to larger, more grandiose homes with each passing decade.

It is said that a man's home is his castle. Or is it? Sometimes, our homes become our prisons, turning us into weekend slaves as we spend time maintaining properties we hardly enjoy because we are working so hard to pay for them. Even if you are rich, it still takes time and energy to hire and supervise the staff to care for your home, or in some cases, your two to four homes. Not only are we using the earth's resources to build homes with space we don't need or use regularly, but we also have to furnish, maintain, and insure this excess space, adding to our cost of living.

Architecture is frozen music.

Madame de Staël

SIMPLICITY AND BEAUTY

Living in a home that is not too big and not too small is important. Another worthwhile endeavor is to grace your home with simplicity and beauty. To experience simplicity in your home, imagine a tall, handsome guard adorned in an impressive uniform, polished boots, and sparkling sword, standing outside your front door. Nothing gets through that front door unless the simplicity guard determines it will serve a valued function or bring you aesthetic pleasure. You and your family get to decide what is beautiful and what is not.

It is wise to invest real thought and caring into your décor; your well-being depends on it. The architectural style and materials used in your home are also important. Don't let a tight budget defeat you; even the smallest, most humble abode can be made beautiful. For example, a single flower in a skinny jar on the dining table can add beauty to a room. This is how one person featured in my book, *Choosing Simplicity*, describes her inexpensive, 900 square-foot home:

> It's so cute, just the right size. It's unique, has nice hardwood floors that are wonderful to wax and polish, very soothing, and very beautiful wooden doors. And I've got photos and mementos from trips all over the walls.

As roads go, the road home is as good as any.

Ellis Peters

You can create a home that communicates serenity and calm or one that speaks of clutter, excess, and chaos. The way you live in your home is an interactive process—it will affect and reflect your personality. So which is it? Do you want to be serene and calm or scattered and out of control?

Bringing simplicity into your home—limiting your furnishings and belongings to only those things you need or cherish—is a challenging but immensely rewarding project. Keep in mind that if you fill every wall and floor space with things, it may be difficult to enjoy very much of it. Try leaving some empty spaces. You may discover you will better notice and appreciate what's left. Whatever your preferred style, whatever your budget, be sure that your home reflects your aesthetic tastes.

RENT OR BUY?

The question of whether to rent or buy a home is, for many, a simple matter of economics. If you can afford it, you buy. If you can't, you rent. After all, isn't home ownership an essential element of the American dream? Some would disagree. They are overwhelmingly enthusiastic about renting rather than owning a home. They cite many reasons, including the freedom to spend their weekends doing things other than house repairs and mowing the lawn.

There are both economic and quality of life factors that determine whether owning or renting a home is the best choice for you and your family.

The economics of home ownership versus renting can be complex. First, you compare rental rates with the cost of home ownership—mortgage payments, taxes, insurance, maintenance, and the often overlooked *opportunity cost* of your down payment money. By opportunity cost, I mean the amount of income you would earn if you invested your down payment money somewhere else. Because you give up that income when you buy a home, you should consider it as a cost of owning the home. If you buy a home outright without a mortgage, then you need to factor in the opportunity cost of the total purchase price.

One economic factor that offsets the costs of home ownership is appreciation. This is where it gets tricky. Traditionally, real estate values in the United States have increased over time. Annual appreciation of existing single-family homes in the United States has averaged approximately four percent during the last 10 years.[4] But appreciation varies depending on the geographical area and how much time is involved. Sometimes home prices stay level or even decrease. If you decide to sell your home within a few years of purchase, you may or may not see any appreciation.

A house is no home unless it contains food and fire for the mind as well as for the body.

Margaret Fuller

When people buy a home, they often believe they will stay in it for a long time. In the United States, the average homeowner moves every eight years, while renters move every two years on average.[5] We are a mobile, changing society. Try to be realistic about how long you will stay in a home. Are you planning to increase your family size? Are you likely to move for better job opportunities? What other factors might influence you to move or stay put? If you are likely to move within a few years of purchase, you may want to rent instead of buy a home, unless you are very confident that your home will appreciate. In any event, it is wise to analyze the relative costs of buying versus renting a home before you make your decision. You will have an opportunity to do this analysis for your present home in the lifework assignments below.

In addition to economics, there are quality of life factors to consider. Apartment living usually means less room to store things we really don't need or want (providing a forced de-cluttering incentive) and less space to clean. Renting eliminates concerns about major maintenance headaches, property taxes, property insurance, and the economic risks of fires, earthquakes, floods, and hurricanes. There is a sense of freedom with renting. You can take off at a moment's notice with less concern about maintenance or landscaping matters. As a renter, if you lose your job and need to reduce your expenses, you can change your housing more easily without suffering further economic losses.

Of course, there are also quality of life benefits to owning a home. If you love to garden, you don't need to get a landlord's permission to change the existing landscaping. Some people have pets, which are rarely popular with landlords. Privacy is often mentioned as a benefit of owning a home. While this is undoubtedly relevant when considering a home versus an apartment, a rented home can offer you the same privacy as one that is purchased.

There are also intangible benefits to owning a home. When you rent, your landlord can kick you out when your lease expires. If you own, you are unlikely to be forced to move (unless your local government decides to build a freeway through your living room).

All things that a man owns hold him far more than he holds them.

Sigrid Undset

People talk about a sense of security and a sense of pride in owning a home. Why do we feel a greater sense of pride in owning a home? It may relate in part to the underlying symbolism we ascribe to home ownership. In North America, home ownership represents a form of status. It's a signal that you have arrived at a certain socio-economic level. Since we are taught that home ownership is an essential part of the American dream, it's no wonder we feel a sense of accomplishment when we buy a home. If, however, our internal pride meter was tied to who we are rather than what we own, we could then base a decision on whether to buy or rent on cost and quality of life factors alone. After all, there is no reason why a renter could not feel the same sense of pride as a homeowner in creating a home of simplicity and beauty.

WHERE AND HOW TO LIVE

Decisions, decisions—big city, suburb, small town, rural, detached or attached home, apartment, condominium, gated community, senior community, cohousing community, downtown high-rise, RV living, houseboat, traditional neighborhood development, mountain cabin, tent or yurt. What did I miss? The choices can be overwhelming. Costs of living, schools, safety, work opportunities, cultural amenities, aesthetic characteristics, weather patterns, proximity to family and friends, and transportation options all factor into the decision.

Your age and family commitments will also influence you. If

you are a college student, your choice may be narrowed to living in a college dormitory or renting an apartment with one or more friends. If you are a young adult, you are more likely to consider a change in location than if you are middle-aged or older and feel rooted in a community or you want to stay put to fulfill family obligations. If you don't want to move, it is still helpful to be conscious of the reasons you live where you do and to affirm that choice for yourself. Remember, simplicity is about living consciously and deliberately. In the sections that follow, you will explore various options of where and how to live.

LIVABLE TOWNS AND CITIES

America has now squandered its national wealth erecting a human habitat that, in all likelihood, will not be usable very much longer, and there are few unspoiled places left to retreat to in the nation's habitable reaches.

James Howard Kunstler

The dominant trend in housing development in the United States during the last 50 years has been suburban growth, also known as urban sprawl. In fact, the percentage of people who live in suburbs doubled from 1900 to 1950 and then doubled again from 1950 to 2000, reaching a current level of over 50 percent of the population.[6]

Suburban life has been criticized for its negative impact on the environment (due primarily to its almost exclusive dependence on the automobile for transportation) and on the loss of community. A new approach to housing and communities is advocated by a number of complementary trends and movements, including the New Urbanism and Smart Growth movements and related organizations.[7] These groups of architects, developers, urban planners, and concerned citizens are exploring alternatives to suburban growth. I refer to these alternatives collectively as *livable towns and cities*. The primary features of livable towns and cities include:

- Mixed residential, commercial, civic, and open space uses are encouraged, all within walking distance (5 to 10 minutes) of each other.
- Automobile traffic is accommodated but does not dominate the landscape. Narrow streets and natural traffic calming devices, such as fountains, curves, and medians, inhibit the speed of traffic. Garages are often placed behind the home (sometimes served by an alley).

- Walking and bicycling for both recreation and transportation are encouraged. Pathways for both are plentiful and safe. (We may also see an increase of other transportation options such as the Segway™ Human Transporter, especially if such vehicles prove to be safe, economically feasible, and environmentally-friendly.)
- A diversified selection of housing—apartments, single-family homes, live/work units, and multi-family dwellings—serves a wide range of ages, lifestyles, and incomes.
- A town center or square provides a setting for informal community interaction, civic functions, and businesses that offer goods and services for daily living.

Landscape shapes culture.

Terry Tempest Williams

- Abundant green spaces supply natural beauty and recreational opportunities.
- Preservation of agricultural and other open lands surrounding the livable town or city is a high priority, accomplished in part by higher density development within the town.
- The aesthetics of the public realm is highly valued for its beneficial impact on psychological well-being, civic pride, and commitment to the community.
- Certain design elements encourage community interaction and an experience of the neighborhood and town as an extension of the home. For example, narrow, attractive, tree-lined streets with ample sidewalks entice people to spend time outside. Homes with front porches positioned at the front of the lot encourage people to engage in casual conversation with passersby. Lots smaller than the typical suburban model allow a greater number of people to live closer to each other, increasing the likelihood that they will interact with each other.
- Ideally, work opportunities are integrated into the community to enable residents to walk, bicycle, or drive a short distance to work.

This model of living requires higher population densities than the suburban way of life. It departs from North American tradition and culture, which has grown up on wide, open spaces. In contrast, European populations tend to cluster in denser, more self-sustaining towns and villages surrounded by open spaces.

The Slow Cities movement in Italy, which evolved from the Slow Food movement, celebrates this tradition and promotes the positive benefits of the small, pedestrian-friendly town. No doubt the differences in Europe are based in part on the fact that the automobile did not exist at the time most European towns and cities were first developed.

Livable towns and neighborhoods in North America are not limited to new developments. Some existing small towns and neighborhoods within larger cities meet the criteria of livable towns. Whether new or old, this form of community supports living more simply, allowing residents to spend less time and money on housing, transportation, and work. Livable towns and cities also offer tremendous benefits in the way we experience time (see discussion in Lesson 5). Opportunities to experience community and preserve natural resources are enhanced in livable towns and cities.

The tragedy [of our time] is that we do not know what we like until we are told by our advertisers and entertainers.

Jessamyn West

Governmental incentives (for example, tax credits or low interest loans) would further development of livable towns and cities. I believe that taxpayers would get a good return on their investment in the form of reduced problems associated with the loss of community and family support. A society with a strong family and community fabric is likely to have fewer problem youths, less crime, less substance abuse, and less unemployment. Environmental costs and damage would decrease with higher density housing models.

This is not to say you can't experience community in a suburb or that the livable town model is ideal for everyone. For example, some prefer a rural environment for work or lifestyle reasons. Others prefer big city living, which often offers excellent resources (cultural, recreational, educational, products, and services) within walking distance. As stated above, certain areas of large cities would qualify as a livable neighborhood. Your goal should be to carefully consider the pros and cons of different lifestyle choices rather than automatically choosing the mainstream North American preference for suburban living.

CREATIVE HOUSING ALTERNATIVES

There is a wide range of alternatives to living as one person or family in a single-family, detached home. Various forms of cohousing and communal living opportunities, ranging from highly structured work/live cooperatives to small, more informal arrangements, are discussed in Lesson 11.

If you are willing to contribute labor in exchange for housing, there are many opportunities for inexpensive housing, such caretaking positions, live-in nanny jobs, and ranch-hand positions.

A man who accustoms himself to buy superfluities, is often in want of necessities.

Hannah Farnham Lee

There is also the potential to share housing but still retain an independent living space. Today, traditional zoning in the United States separates uses—single-family, multi-family, commercial, and industrial. A small change in this direction could be made by allowing *granny flat* units in single-family residence zones. These secondary units are typically created by building an apartment over the garage or carving out a separate section of a home to be rented to someone else. Some people take their master bedroom suite, add a small kitchenette and a separate entrance, and rent out this space as a studio unit.

Or you could reverse the process, especially if you are single. Rent out the bulk of your home to a paying tenant and live in a portion you have reserved for yourself. This could be an excellent means to finance travel, take a sabbatical, or reduce your working hours.

Expanding zoning uses within a geographical area could also open up possibilities for seniors who continue to live in large homes after their children have moved out. Some may feel lost in so much space, but don't want to move. If zoning laws allowed splitting that home into two or three living units, the owners could stay in their home and have close neighbors.

These are just a few ideas to get you thinking. In the lesson assignments below, you will have the opportunity to dream up your own creative alternatives to housing.

ECONOMIC INCENTIVES

In Lesson 2, we looked at levying an *earth tax* on the consumption of non-essential items as a *pay-as-you-go* contribution to the earth's diminishing resources. Similarly, we could ask our government to impose an earth tax on homes of an excessive size. Obviously, there would be significant political and practical obstacles to implementing such a tax. I raise this idea theoretically as a starting point for further thought and discussion.

The objective here is to explore how we might live in greater harmony with the earth. We've already considered other more personal, less altruistic reasons why living in a home that is not too big and not too small makes sense.

Let's assume that we North Americans were committed to reducing our utilization of the earth's resources to something more akin to what our population warrants. Let's also assume that we don't want to force people to live in smaller homes. By implementing an earth tax, we ask those who choose to use more than their fair share of the earth's resources to contribute to ameliorating the damage. We could use those tax proceeds for technological and other solutions to reduce human-caused damage to the earth.

We're all born brave, trusting, and greedy, and most of us remain greedy.

Mignon McLaughlin

Next, let's assume North Americans could agree on a *reasonable* size for a home. Since reasonability would obviously depend in part on the number of people in a household, we might calculate this figure as the amount of square feet per resident. Let's also assume that there would be a reasonable amount of additional square feet allocated for rooms used primarily for business activities or active, space-intensive hobbies. If we establish a certain benchmark—hypothetically, for example, 500 square feet per person, not including space used primarily for business or active hobbies—we could then require people who live in homes larger than the agreed-upon standard to pay an earth tax. So, in this hypothetical example, if a family of four lived in a 3,000 square-foot home and did not engage in any at-home businesses or active hobbies, they would pay an earth tax for the additional 1,000 square feet over the reasonable allotment (500 square feet multiplied by four people).

Some would view such an earth tax as a penalty. The rich might feel they have worked hard for their money and should not be penalized if they can afford a larger home than the average North American. But if we view the tax as a fair contribution to the earth's diminishing resources rather than a penalty, it loses some of its sting.

In addition to levying an earth tax on housing that places an excessive burden on the earth, we could offer earth tax credits for housing that minimizes natural resources, such as homes built of straw bale, rammed earth, adobe, and cob. One obstacle to the widespread use of such materials is the prevalence of restrictive building codes. Since these building forms are still relatively rare, many municipalities have not incorporated them into their building codes. Hopefully, this will change with greater education and awareness of the earth's environmental condition.

If we would have new knowledge, we must get us a whole world of new questions.

Susanne K. Langer

I present these alternatives as a starting point, as a trigger to stimulate your own thoughts and ideas on what economic incentives might encourage people to refrain from living beyond the earth's means. In the lesson assignments that follow, you will have the opportunity to do just that.

CONCLUSION

One of the most significant decisions we make in life is where and how we live. For most of us, this will change from time to time. Our choices have far reaching impacts. Our homes affect our sense of well-being, influence our choices about work (based on the cost of our housing), and determine to some extent the quality of our community experiences. It is our choice and responsibility to create a home, however humble or small, that serves as a comforting retreat, an environment that allows us to center ourselves before venturing out into the world again.

The choices in housing styles and locations are vast. Having a limited budget is no excuse for living in a home that does not nurture you. However, it can take a lot of work, imagination, and flexibility to create a home environment that's just right for you. Go for it!

LESSON ASSIGNMENTS

FROM YOUR PERSONAL VIEWPOINT . . .

1. Calculate the size of your home in square feet per household member. If you own your home, you can often find the total square footage in the marketing materials related to the purchase of your home. If you rent your home or apartment, your landlord is likely to know the total square footage. If you use certain rooms for an at-home business or active hobbies, first deduct a reasonable square footage for those rooms from the total square feet. Then, divide the balance by the number of people living in your home. For example, if your home is 2,200 square feet (after deducting any square footage for business uses) and you have three people in your family, your home size is 733 square feet per family member. How do you feel about the size of your home? Is it too big, too small, or just right?
2. If you feel your home is too big, would you consider carving out some portion of it to rent to another? Or would you possibly be interested in moving to a smaller home?
3. Are there rooms in your home that give you a sense of simplicity and beauty and others that do not? Try to identify what it is in these rooms that contribute to your experience (or lack of) of simplicity and beauty. What changes would bring greater simplicity and beauty into your home?
4. How do you feel about your neighborhood and the town or city you live in? Is it aesthetically pleasing? How easy or difficult is it, transportation-wise, to meet your daily needs? Do you engage in your desired level of community involvement? What are the pros and cons of where you live?
5. Describe your ideal home environment—size, style, aesthetics, neighborhood, and town. Be as detailed as you can.

The only questions that really matter are the ones you ask yourself.

Ursula K. Le Guin

LOOKING AT THE BIGGER PICTURE . . .

6. Think of new ways of living for people in your country. If you live in North America, consider models that would

increase community and decrease environmental burdens. If you live elsewhere, what is your vision of an ideal form of housing and community? Think creatively and, at this point, don't let the practical challenges of implementing your vision limit your imagination. Be as detailed as possible.

7. What social and public policies would encourage people to live in a *not so big house*? What standards would best be used to determine an appropriately sized home?

LIFEWORK ASSIGNMENTS

Can't nothin' make your life work if you ain't the architect.

Terry McMillan

1. Calculate the economic factors in renting versus owning the house or apartment you live in. The *Buy Versus Rent Analysis* on page 202 outlines the factors you need to consider in your calculation. You can simply substitute your own numbers into this chart to complete your analysis.
2. Determine the amount of time you spend operating your home (either directly or by supervising others), including tasks related to maintenance, insurance, landscaping, repairs, and improvements. Are you at all surprised at the results?
3. If you would like to make a change in your choice of a home or town, start researching your options. Use the Internet and the resources listed below to explore possibilities. Don't feel you need to make this change in the next six months. It often takes one to three years to implement major changes to the infrastructure of our lives. Try not to feel overwhelmed with the project. It can all be done in small steps over a period of time. The first step is research.

ANNUAL CHECK-UP

1. Have your space needs for housing changed in the last year? Do you have new members in your family or have some members moved on? What about other space needs—work or other projects done at home? If your needs have changed, does your home still suit you? If not, start

exploring other alternatives.

2. Have you made any progress with adding simplicity and beauty to your home? What more do you want to do, if anything?
3. What about the location of your home? Does it meet your needs for ease of living, community interaction, aesthetics, cultural opportunities, and proximity to work? Have any of these needs changed for you during the last year?
4. If you decided last year to make a change in your home or town, what progress have you made so far? Have you refined your vision as a result of the research you did? What do you want to accomplish towards this goal in the following year?

RECOMMENDED RESOURCES

Books

Carrying Water as a Way of Life: A Homesteader's History by Linda Tatelbaum (Appleton, ME: About Time Press, 1997). Memoir of a homesteading lifestyle in rural Maine.

Moving to a Small Town: A Guidebook for Moving from Urban to Rural America by Wanda Urbanska and Frank Levering (New York: Simon & Schuster, 1996). This practical and anecdotal guide on moving to a small town includes tips on scouting a location, planning the move, calculating the costs, remaking a career in a rural area, and fitting into a new community.

The New Apartment Book by Michele Michael (New York: Clarkson N. Potter, December 1996). This book offers tips and guidelines on decorating an apartment to create a stylish home in limited space on a middle-class budget.

The Not So Big House: A Blueprint for the Way We Really Live by Sarah Susanka (Newtown, CT: The Taunton Press, 1998). Best-selling architect/author argues that what we really want in housing are informal, beautiful, cozy spaces that serve the functions we do in the home rather than large, formal rooms that look more like museums than homes.

Suburban Nation: The Rise of Sprawl and the Decline of the American Dream by Andres Duany, Elizabeth Plater-Zyberk and Jeff Speck (New York: North Point Press, 2001). New urbanist planners outline the devastating effects of post-war suburban sprawl on communities and social health. They advocate a return to the traditional neighborhoods planning style of mixed use, pedestrian-friendly communities.

MISCELLANEOUS

The Caretaker Gazette [www.caretaker.org] is a bimonthly newsletter containing property caretaking and housesitting opportunities, advice, and information for property caretakers, housesitters, and landowners.

Congress for the New Urbanism [www.cnu.org] is a membership organization of architects, planners, and developers who support the new urbanism movement. Its web site includes a database of livable towns and cities.

Earthstar Primal Habitat Project [www.geocities.com/~newliberty/earthstar] is the work of Kevin and Donna Philippe-Johnson. This web site details the couple's experience of building a B.E.L.L. (Biogenic Ecodesic Living Lighthouse pioneered by Edmond Bordeaux Szekely) home and their experiences of living a simple, primal lifestyle that minimizes the use of natural resources.

Habitat for Humanity [www.habitat.org] is an international, nonprofit, nondenominational Christian organization whose volunteers build affordable housing in partnership with those in need in 80 countries throughout the world.

The *Slow Cities* movement [www.slowfood.com/eng/sf_ita_mondo/sf_ita_citta_slow.lasso] is an offshoot of the *Slow Food* movement. Its members are towns and cities (most of which are located in Italy) that value quality of life for its residents, with an emphasis on leisurely meals, community involvement, pedestrian and bicycle friendly towns, environmental sustainability, aesthetic beauty, and reduction of noise and pollution.

NOTE: *Additions and updates to these resources can be found on The Simplicity Resource Guide at www.gallagherpress.com/pierce.*

LESSON 5

Where Did All the Time Go?

WHAT IS TIME, ANYWAY?

"Time and space," author Edith Nesbitt said, "are only forms of thought." Certainly she is right in some respects. Unlike matter, we cannot touch, see, hear, or smell time. Why then do we long to possess it? Time expands and contracts, according to our moods and activities. It often slips away silently and unobtrusively, catching us by surprise. Do we ever have enough of it?

We in the modern world place a high premium on time, measuring it even by nanoseconds as we plot our ways through life. But it wasn't always this way, nor were we always servants of the tyrant time. In her book, *Ohitika Woman*, Mary Brave Bird explains, "There is Indian time and white man's time. Indian time means never looking at the clock. . . . There is not even a word for time in our language."

In fact, time is a human artifice, a symbolic measurement of the earth's cycles from day to night and from one season to another. While the earth knows only cyclical time, we humans have devised a linear construct of time in which we measure not only the earth's cycles but also a cumulative sequence of those cycles, represented in months and years. By doing so, we experience time as finite. The fact that we inhabit this earth for a short period of time reinforces our sense of time as valuable and limited.

When we view time in this way, it is surely our greatest and, in many respects, our only personal asset. Everything else—our money, our possessions, our health, our loved ones—can be taken from our lives, sometimes suddenly and without warning. But we all have the same 24 hours a day—no more, no less—as long as we live on this earth.

Our experience of time is highly subjective. Two people can spend the same amount of time in one activity but experience it quite differently. One may feel rushed and harried while the other feels relaxed and unhurried. For one, time may seem to elongate, while it appears to shrink for another. It is not just the raw number of hours that we crave. We yearn for the experience of feeling present, being fully engaged in whatever we are doing (or not doing) without feeling the pressure and distraction of other responsibilities or interests. This state of mind is known as mindfulness.

When we are in a state of mindfulness, time stands still. We are blissfully unaware of the passage of time. We may only realize that time has passed at some later point when we observe that the morning or day has gone by in a flash. So, while we tell ourselves we want to *find* more time, what we really want to do is *lose* more time—to experience more moments of forgetting that time exists. Some athletes and performers have described this experience as being in the *zone*.

Each moment in time we have it all, even when we think we don't.

Melody Beattie

Moreover, we want to spend our time well, meaning that we want to spend it doing things we value and enjoy. After all, time measures our lives and we want our lives to count.

WHERE DID THE TIME GO?

It's ironic: today we North Americans have more time-saving devices and less time than ever. In addition to adding a full month to our annual work hours in the last 50 years,[1] we have expanded our expectations of what we can accomplish in a 24-hour day. The pace of our lives has evolved from the ambling roll of a pioneer wagon to the whizzing blur of a high-speed commuter train. Life in the fast lane extends to all classes and ages, even to children. The average child today could use a Day-Timer® or Palm Pilot™ to keep track of his schedule. When I grew up in a family of 10 in the 1950's and 1960's, one letter-sized wall calendar served the entire family. How many families could do that today?

In his book *Timeshifting*, Stephan Rechtschaffen explains that through the process of *entrainment*, we have a tendency to align our personal rhythms with those of our environment. So, if we are surrounded by people who are talking fast, walking fast, and working fast, we are likely to do the same. If we listen to loud rock music, we are likely to want to dance, not fall asleep. If we immerse ourselves in nature, surrounded by peaceful vistas and melodic bird singing, we are likely to feel calm.

Another explanation for our supercharged culture is that we are addicted to the frenzied pace. When we dash from one activity to another, consumed with multi-tasking, we experience a surge of adrenaline. We may feel an enhanced sense of importance because we are so busy. For a while we're on an artificial high, with no let down where we might feel bored or depressed.

While this adrenaline rush may feel good momentarily, it's like any other addiction. Eventually we crash. A fast-paced lifestyle depletes us physically, emotionally, and mentally. And then what? Like all addicts, we seek more stimulation. And the cycle continues. This destructive cycle, year after year, interferes with our personal relationships, dulls our brains, and eventually robs us of our zest for life.

This tendency to be doing, doing, doing rather than just being is widespread in North America and, increasingly, in other western cultures. Not surprisingly, even as our levels of productivity and efficiency multiply, we report that we suffer from time deprivation. Two-thirds of Americans say that having more time with family and friends is critical to their being more satisfied with their lives.[2] As discussed above, it is the ability to experience the present moment—to pay attention to what we are doing, thinking, and feeling—that allows us to live as if time were infinite. A fast-paced lifestyle prevents us from living mindfully.

Even the worst blizzard of the century accumulates one flake at a time.

Mary Kay Blakely

CULTIVATING MINDFULNESS, EXPANDING TIME

So how do we create more mindfulness and time in our lives? Unlike money, you cannot win a time lottery. No one can give you more time. It's up to you to create it for yourself. You can make major structural changes—possibly downsizing work hours or moving to a smaller, easy-to-maintain home closer to your work—or smaller, less dramatic modifications. Some adjustments will take a year or more to accomplish. Others you can start on today.

The first step is self-knowledge. We need to know how we spend our time now. Of course, we think we already know that, but most people who take an inventory of their time are surprised at the results. Later in this lesson you will have the opportunity to do your own time inventory. This exercise is similar to tracking the money that comes into and goes out of your life.

We will not only track how much time we spend on various activities, but will also rate the relative value of those activities. Awareness by itself is likely to lead you to make positive changes. Clear evidence that you spend time on activities of little value to you provides the incentive to make new choices.

There are a number of small changes you can implement to slow the pace of your life. Start to observe when and why you feel deprived of time. Are there certain activities or times of the day when you feel a particular time crunch? Some people feel squeezed too tightly for time before and after work. They mentally set aside 8 to 10 hours (including commute time) for work, but experience the hours before or after work as chaotic and stressful.

I have learned to live each day as it comes, and not to borrow trouble by dreading tomorrow.

Dorothy Dix

You may be able to shift certain activities to reduce the chaotic time periods in your day. For example, a person who exercises before work may choose to do it during her lunch break instead, which in turn allows her to enjoy a more relaxed morning routine. Perhaps she can negotiate an extended lunch break with her employer—possibly in exchange for adding an additional 30 minutes to the end of her work day—so she doesn't replace a chaotic morning with a time-stressed lunch period. Another option would be to go to sleep a half-hour earlier, and then get up that much earlier to expand the pre-work hours.

One seemingly obvious (yet incredibly difficult) tool to master is the ability to say no. This takes practice. Let's say a friend calls to invite you for dinner on Friday night. You look at your calendar and Friday is wide open. But you also notice that you have activities planned for both Saturday and Sunday. This is a time to use restraint. Just say no. You need *down* time—time to hang out by yourself or with your family. You can simply tell your friend, "Gee, I'm sorry, but I have another commitment." This is not a lie. You do have another commitment—a commitment to yourself to live a balanced life. How many social events can you handle each week and still have enough *down* time? For me, two evenings a week is about right. If I schedule much more than that, I start to feel a little off-centered.

The ability to say *no, thank you* is even more critical for those activities we would not want to do even if we had unlimited time. Are there people with whom you socialize just because it's a habit and not because you still enjoy their company? What about volunteer activities? Are you committing time to projects that are enjoyable and meaningful, or are you acting from a feeling of guilt? Be sure that your time commitments reflect your authentic desires.

Sometimes we enjoy certain activities but fail to keep them in balance. For instance, do you subscribe to magazines you don't have time to read, and then feel guilty when you don't read them all? Consider reducing your subscriptions to one or two, and then add others gradually if and when you read the ones you already have. Take some time to sit with each of your magazines and ask yourself what it actually contributes to your life. If the answer is nothing, drop your subscription.

To live exhilaratingly in and for the moment is deadly serious work, fun of the most exhausting sort.

Barbara Grizzuti Harrison

When you are tempted to add something new to your life—a new friend, volunteer opportunity, or whatever—ask yourself what you are willing to give up to make room for this new addition. Often we take on new opportunities, causes, or adventures based on their own merits without realizing that to make room for the new, some of the old must go. Be conscious of the choices that affect your time—it's your most precious asset. Learn to say no if the value isn't there.

One technique to soften a frenetic lifestyle is to schedule *surround* time. This is the time that surrounds your activities. For example, let's say you plan to meet a friend for coffee after a dental appointment. You expect to leave the dentist's office at 3:00 P.M. and walk 10 minutes to the café where you will meet your friend. Instead of scheduling your rendezvous for 3:15 P.M., schedule it for 3:30 P.M. This will give you 15 to 20 minutes of *surround* time between your two appointments. Surround time gives you freedom. For example, you might want to have a spontaneous five-minute chat with the receptionist on your way out of the dental office. If you find that your route is blocked off for construction and you need to detour a few blocks, you will not fret about being late. Or you could purposely take a longer route to enjoy the gardens on a particular street. Life is filled with surprises and opportunities. Plan for them.

If you arrive 15 minutes earlier than your friend, you get a bonus of *found* time, a period of time to just be—to relax, daydream, or watch people. Think of this state as mental hang gliding. If you're uncomfortable with just being, you can always carry some reading material with you. By scheduling surround time, you tell your brain that time is *not* in short supply. If you send this message to your brain often, it will start to believe it.

Consider planning for spontaneity. No, this is not an oxymoron. You can purposefully leave plenty of time for spontaneous events to occur. For example, if you want to spend the day hiking with a friend and then meet a few co-workers for dinner, schedule these two events on different days. You never know what could happen after a day in the woods or walking at the seashore.

We are drowning in information but starved for knowledge.

John Naisbitt

INFORMATION OVERLOAD

Information overload is the nemesis of mindfulness. We can easily be overwhelmed and over-stimulated by the volume of information and entertainment available to us. When we subject ourselves to information overload, we cannot slow our minds down sufficiently to focus on what we are doing. Consequently, we read the newspaper while eating breakfast and watch a tiny kitchen TV while cooking dinner. As discussed above, we have a tendency to synchronize our internal rhythms with our environment. If you expose your mind to constant outside stimulation, spending every spare moment watching television or surfing the Internet, your brain will struggle to adjust to a slower, less scattered rhythm.

If you suffer from information overload, try reducing the overall stimulation in your life gradually. For example, if your commute includes drive time or a train ride, let your mind float in neutral rather than listen to the radio or read every minute. This can be difficult, especially if you're accustomed to constant media bombardment. You might have to start slowly, taking short mental hang gliding breaks at first, and then increasing the duration. Eventually you might try a media fast, described in the lifework assignments below.

SWEEPING FLOORS, WASHING DISHES

Physical chores offer excellent opportunities for practicing mindfulness, as they generally do not require intense mental effort. I've heard more than one person speak about the simple pleasure of washing dishes—feeling the warm, sudsy water and the satisfaction of turning dirty dishes into clean ones with relatively little effort. (Don't we wish all our work activities produced such tangible results?) There is something inherently very satisfying about working with our hands and moving our bodies. Focusing on these activities as we are doing them will bring that feeling of satisfaction to the surface of your consciousness.

To survive we must begin to know sacredness. The pace which most of us live prevents this.

Chrystos

Consider a scene in a movie in which the camera focuses on a character performing a seemingly mundane chore in such a way as to elevate the task to one of great beauty and meaning. Of course, the background music helps to create the mood. Some of the well-known food films, such as *Like Water for Chocolate* and *Babette's Feast*, come to mind. Next time you prepare food for a meal, imagine the camera, music, and lighting spotlighting your activity, recording your every move. It can give you a feeling that what you are doing is very important, even though it may not be seen by anyone other than your dog sitting at your feet waiting for you to drop some scraps on the floor.

This exercise will help you develop a sense of what it is to live in the present. By focusing on the activity itself, giving it your full attention, you bring yourself into the present, where time disappears.

WORKING FEWER HOURS

As we have seen, there is much we can do as individuals to alter our experience of time. On a societal level, there is also much that can be done to expand time for individuals and families. Social and public policies that enable work/life balance are essential for this purpose.

In the United States, there was a legislative proposal in the 1930's to reduce the standard work hours to 30 hours per week. The Senate passed the bill but the House killed it. Since the

1950's, we have added a full month to our total annual work hours.[3] In 1997, the United States had the dubious distinction of surpassing Japan as the industrialized country with the greatest number of annual hours worked, reaching nearly 2,000 hours per year.[4]

Approximately 37 percent of full-time, salaried Americans work 50 or more hours per week.[5] People in most European countries work 15 to 20 percent fewer work hours (equivalent to nine weeks!) than Americans.[6]

Perhaps it is time to reexamine our standards in this regard. The simple truth is that if we work 40, 50, or 60 hours a week—either to achieve career success or to pay for our chosen standard of living—we will not have the time and energy to invest in quality relationships, healthful living, inner simplicity, connecting to nature, and community participation.

The road to happiness lies in an organized diminution of work.

Bertrand Russell

Certainly, some people have high energy levels and can comfortably balance a full-time job with a life outside of work. But they are in the minority and tend to be young and single. If you are 24-years old and just starting out in your career, you may be tempted to work 60 to 80 hours a week. However, if you keep up that pace over many years, you will become a one-dimensional person defined by your work, with scant experience as a full human being.

North American culture is so imbued with a strong work ethic that working fewer hours—or at least doing something *productive* with our time—is seen as almost sacrilegious. That is why we often feel guilty if we *waste* time. The initial growth of America can be credited to hard-working, determined pioneers whose survival was at stake. Undoubtedly, we have inherited some of that pioneer drive and strength. But basic survival for most of us is no longer at issue. We can relax a little. We don't have to work as much as we do to meet our basic physical needs.

Let's examine what some would consider a radical proposal—reducing the standard work week from 40 to 30 hours. Critics of reduced work hours cite the negative economic impacts of such a policy. Who will take the hit? Will the employee's salary be decreased by 25 percent or will employers absorb a 25 percent decrease in productivity?

It may be that neither party will need to take such a loss. If we implement a reduction of work hours over a period of years, it would lessen the economic blow to both the employer and the employee. One approach would be for employers to reduce work hours by one hour a week over a period of 10 years (resulting in a 30-hour work week) in exchange for employees giving up salary increases during that same 10-year period. Surveys indicate that while people believe they can't live on less income, many would choose more time over money if given the choice[7].

Many employers have found that employee productivity does not decrease hour for hour when work hours are reduced. Since employees will be less tired and stressed on a reduced schedule, they are likely to be more productive on an hourly basis. Also, time spent on personal phone calls, email, and medical appointments during work hours would likely decrease because employees would have more personal time to accomplish these tasks. Some experts in work productivity claim that 50 percent of the reduction in work hours is offset by increased hourly productivity.[8]

Too much safety is abhorrent to the nature of a human being.

Agatha Christie

Potential productivity losses from reduced work hours will also be offset by cost savings in hiring and training new employees. Since workers are likely to stay longer in jobs that permit work/life balance, employee turnover rate should decrease.

One obstacle to persuading employers to reduce work hours relates to the structure of benefit programs. Typically, an employer pays a fixed health insurance premium whether the employee works 25 or 50 hours a week. The employer may resist dividing a 50-hour per week job into two positions if it means doubling its cost for health insurance. On the other hand, as discussed above, those two 25-hours per week employees are likely to produce the equivalent of 60 or more hours of work, resulting in a decreased benefit cost per hour worked.

As a society, if we shift the cost of certain employee benefits, such as health insurance, from employers to taxpayers, there would be less incentive for employers to maximize the number of hours per worker. Moreover, if employers were no longer responsible for health insurance, this might offset their potential losses in productivity. The increased burden on taxpayers would be mitigated to some degree by reduced governmental costs for unemployment and social assistance programs.

Another perceived obstacle to reducing work hours from an employer's point of view is overhead costs. For example, a company who employs 50 office workers may have 50 office workstations. If it reduces work hours by 25 percent over a period of time, it may need to hire an additional 8 to 12 people to produce the same amount of work, which would in theory require the employer to purchase the same number of additional workstations.

But there is another approach that would better serve the employer, the environment, and society: let the overhead put in a double shift. For example, some employees who work a six-hour day could work from 6:00 a.m. to 2:00 p.m. while others would work from 2:00 p.m. to 8:00 p.m. This could be beneficial to families with children whose parents want time to spend with their children or attend their children's school activities. It allows employees to conduct personal business—doctor's appointments, visits to the bank, miscellaneous errands—during business hours without interfering with their work commitments. Moreover, with increasing power of technology—computers, cell phones, video conferencing, etcetera—employees could telecommute by working at home. Finally, fewer workstations results in fewer natural resources taken from the earth.

Satisfaction isn't so much getting what you want as wanting what you have.

David G. Myers

Reduction of weekly work hours is not the only means to provide greater work/life balance. For example, taking a three-month to one-year sabbatical, whether paid or not, is highly likely to restore balance in a person's life. An employee is likely to return from a sabbatical feeling rejuvenated, which in turn, will benefit the employer.

From the employee's point of view, it's true that foregoing salary increases would impact his ability to improve his standard of living—at least in the material realm. But what about quality of life? Too often, we equate standard of living with quality of life when, in fact, they are distinct concepts that sometimes contradict each other. Giving up the possibility of a larger, more expensive home or luxurious vacations could be worthwhile trades for something more valuable—the opportunity to live a balanced lifestyle.

Of course, there would be trickle-down economic impacts flowing from the lack of growth in personal income. Housing values would not appreciate as much. Overall retail growth would slow. We need to ask ourselves as a society whether we want to trade a potential growth in standard of living for an increase in quality of life. This is what is at stake here.

At the time of this writing, a national campaign called *Take Back Your Time*[9] is scheduled for the fall of 2003. On October 24th, the first *Take Back Your Time Day*, thousands of people will take back some of their time by working less or not at all. On that day, hundreds of teach-ins at colleges and other community events will launch a public dialogue about work/life balance. If you are interested in participating in one of these events, you can get further information at the *Take Back Your Time* campaign web site [www.timeday.org].

Happiness consists in the full employment of our faculties in some pursuit.

Harriet Martineau

WORKING THROUGH RETIREMENT

A recent television news show featured people in their 80's and 90's who tried retirement, hated it, and are now back working full-time. It may be that these people failed to develop a life outside of work before retirement and were predictably bored when they did retire. Even so, an argument can be made that the cultural norm of retiring completely at age 65 (assuming we are still mentally and physically capable of working) is outdated and serves neither the individual nor society.

Another vision is possible. Instead of working too many hours in stressful jobs for 45 years, then retiring to a life of boredom, we could work fewer hours for a longer period of time. For example, rather than work 40 hours a week for 45 years, a person might work 30 hours a week for 60 or so years. Society realizes the same productivity benefit (defined as total hours worked) and the individual has a greater quality of life both before and after age 65.

IT'S ALL UP TO YOU

So where does all this leave you? It may take years for the cultural and political forces in North America to adopt a reduced work hours standard. But you don't need to wait for systemic changes to pave the way. You can work part-time now. Maybe not tomorrow, but with planning and foresight, within the next one to two years.

Many people tell themselves they have no choice. They believe they need two full-time workers in the family to pay the bills. So, how is it that thousands of people in North America work part-time and don't feel deprived of material comforts? It can be done. Read the life stories I've written about in *Choosing Simplicity* if you doubt it.

Working part-time is possible if you reduce your living expenses to accommodate a lower income. You need to reexamine your housing, transportation, and consumer spending patterns to see where you can cut back. You can use the Money Worksheet on page 198 to get started. It may take a move to a less expensive home. If you live where some members of your household can walk, ride a bicycle, or take public transportation, you may be able to manage with just one car. Sometimes working at home part-time will put more money into your bank account than working full-time in a traditional job with its associated costs of commuting, dining in restaurants, and a more expensive wardrobe.

Time collapses
and expands like an erratic accordion.

Bel Kaufman

LIVABLE TOWNS AND CITIES

In Lesson 4, we reviewed the concept of livable towns and cities. This urban planning movement values small communities where people can walk to meet most of their daily needs, such as food and household shopping, dining in restaurants, banking, or visits to the library. Civic and recreational destinations are also within a five to ten-minute walking distance.

Obviously, spending 5 to 10 minutes walking rather than 15 to 30 minutes driving saves time. But even if we exchange a ten-minute drive for a ten-minute walk, our brains will think we have more time at our disposal.

To understand how we experience the same 10 minutes as additional time if we walk, we refer again to the concept of mindfulness. Clearly, if you walk rather than drive to a destination, your pace will be slower. With a slower pace, your senses react to your environment more fully. You will be more conscious of the surrounding sights, sounds, and smells. You experience your body and nature in a more direct way—breathing fresh air, your feet touching the ground. Have you ever been surprised to discover new sights when walking a route you normally drive? This direct experience with your environment leads you to be more fully engaged, more present, in what you are doing. As discussed above, it is the act of being present that gives us the sense that time is infinite.

Other factors contribute to your ability to be present when you walk rather than drive a car. Walking is more relaxing than driving or even riding in a car as a passenger. You don't need to focus as much on safety (assuming you are walking on a sidewalk and not on the edge of a busy, narrow road).

Walking is both a form of transportation and exercise. If you are car-dependent for transportation and spend 30 minutes a day in the gym, you can *save* that gym time (not to mention the money for membership fees) if you live in a town where you might walk 30 minutes a day for transportation.

What we lack is not so much leisure to do as time to reflect and time to feel.

Margaret Mead
and Rhoda Metraux

There are substantial time savings in livable towns and cities for families with children. Parents can give up their part-time chauffeuring jobs in such communities. Children can replace boring time spent in the car with pure fun—walking, running, bicycling, scooting about town.

Even if you don't live where you can walk to meet most of your daily needs, perhaps you can still incorporate some walking into your life. For example, if you take the train to work, what about walking to and from the train station? If you need to drive into town for errands, what about walking to each destination once you arrive? Or you could park your car as far as possible from the places you plan to visit. Walking is a basic human function. It slows down our rhythms, connects us to the earth, and provides valuable exercise.

CONCLUSION

People who live simply know the beauty of restraint. Their lives manifest the principle that time is indeed their greatest asset. Their activities reflect the high quality of their lives. They live near their work, keeping commute time to a minimum. They spend quality time in joyful relationships with family and close friends—talking, laughing, cooking, and sharing meals. They do not fill every leisure moment with structured activity.

North Americans can choose to reduce their work hours collectively, as a matter of policy, or individually, as a matter of choice. They can decide to gradually replace suburban sprawl with livable towns and cities. These changes would have profound effects on society as a whole, including reduced health care costs, greater community involvement, and improved parenting. While public policy changes are needed to realize these impacts on a broad scale, the life stories in *Choosing Simplicity* are living testaments that it can be done individually by those who have the confidence and courage to do so.

The way we spend our days is the way we spend our lives.

Annie Dillard

LESSON ASSIGNMENTS

FROM YOUR PERSONAL VIEWPOINT . . .

1. Complete the Time Inventory Worksheet on page 200. Enter your actual estimated hours, the rating for each activity, and your ideal hours' allocation as noted on the form.
2. Think about what you learned from preparing the Time Inventory worksheet. Were there any surprises? Are you pleased with how you spend your time? If not, what areas do you feel are out of balance?
3. Write down 10 things you would do if you had more leisure in your life. How much time do you spend on each of them now?
4. Consider ways in which you could shift your lifestyle more toward the model of your ideal hours. Identify both short-term and long-term solutions. Be creative and wild. Dream big. Write down as many ideas as you can.
5. Do you sometimes have the experience of losing all sense of time? What are you doing when this happens? Describe what this feels like.
6. How do you feel when you are doing household manual chores, such as cleaning, cooking, gardening, or maintenance tasks? Do you enjoy doing them or do you feel bored or burdened by them? What other factors influence your experience of working with your hands and body? For example, if you work with others, does it change the ex-

perience? Does the amount of time you have to do the chore make a difference?

LOOKING AT THE BIGGER PICTURE . . .

7. What are the biggest time-busters in our society? What contributes to our spending time on low priority activities?
8. Consider the implications of a public policy that favors reduced work hours. What are the pros and cons? How would such a policy best be implemented? How could it benefit you?
9. What other social and public policies might have a positive impact on how time is experienced? Describe such policies in as much detail as you can.

To do anything, it is first necessary to be doing nothing.

Nancy Hale

LIFEWORK ASSIGNMENTS

1. For one week, observe when and why you feel time deprived. Keep notes of these times. Becoming aware of your experience of time deprivation is your first step to creating time abundance.
2. Take one activity of low value in your Time Inventory and replace it with a high-value activity. It may only be an hour a week, but it is a start.
3. Take a *down* day—live an entire day with no plans. Just do what you feel like when you feel like it. Live that day without any expectations of doing any particular thing.
4. Leave your watch at home when you don't really need it. For example, if you plan to go to a movie and then return home with no other plans, you don't need a watch. Or try to go an entire day without wearing a watch.
5. Try a media fast for one week. During that week, refrain from watching television, listening to the radio, and reading newspapers and magazines. At the end of your media fast, write down how you felt about it, what it was like, and consider how much media stimulation you want to reintroduce into your life.
6. If you find yourself spending time regularly with people or in activities that are not high value to you, try this exer-

cise. First, figure out what time you need for your top priorities—your work and commuting time, time with your family, time for solitude, daily exercise, sleep, meals, and necessary chores. If you have a strong passion or hobby, you may want to include that activity in your list of top priorities. Then determine how much time you have left for other interests, people, and activities each week. So, for example, you might conclude that you have only 10 hours of discretionary time a week. Then make a commitment not to schedule yourself beyond that amount of time.

There is always time for a nap.

Suzy Becker

ANNUAL CHECK-UP

1. Complete the annual Time Inventory Worksheet on page 200. Compare how you are spending your time with the results from the previous year. Are you getting closer to your ideal?
2. Set some specific goals for the following year to move you closer to your ideal. Be specific and set realistic goals.

RECOMMENDED RESOURCES

BOOKS

Breathing Space: Living and Working at a Comfortable Pace in a Sped-Up Society by Jeff Davidson (Chapel Hill, NC: Breathing Space Institute, Revised 2000). Explores the complex life of the typical, working North American—too rushed and harried, overwhelmed with too many choices, working too many hours, and insufficient sleep. Suggests ways to create more breathing space by taking responsibility for how you spend your time and what you allow to be a part of your environment.

Sharing the Work, Sparing the Planet: Work Time, Consumption, & Ecology by Anders Hayden (London: Zed Books, 2000). Discusses how work time reduction can contribute to reducing persistent unemployment and environmental degradation in industrial societies. Describes a range of possibilities, including a shorter working week, early retirement and parental leave. Explores political, economic, and cultural obstacles to work time reduction.

Six Months Off: How to Plan, Negotiate, and Take the Break You Need without Burning Bridges or Going Broke by Hope Dlugozima, James Scott, and David Sharp (New York: Henry Holt, 1996). Comprehensive guide for taking a sabbatical, including advice on making a proposal to your employer, health insurance alternatives, and financing issues.

Slowing Down in a Speeded Up World by Adair Lara (Berkeley: Conari Press, 1994). Collection of essays, anecdotes, and inspirational quotes on how to bring a sense of calm and peacefulness to our hectic, modern lives.

Take Back Your Time by John de Graaf et al. (San Francisco: Berrett-Koehler, September, 2003). A collection of essays written by prominent writers, university professors, social and environmental activists, business leaders, and physicians on the devastating effects of, and creative solutions to, excessive work hours in North America. Also provides guidelines for organizing community events for Take Back Your Time Day, the first of which is scheduled for October 24, 2003.

Taking Time Off: Inspiring Stories of Students Who Enjoyed Successful Breaks from College and How You Can Plan Your Own by Colin Hall and Ron Lieber (New York: Noonday Press, 1996). Relates stories of college students who have taken breaks before, during, or after college to experience a broad range of alternatives, including community service, living in foreign countries, and non-traditional work experiences. Includes practical guidance on planning a break from college.

The Time Bind: When Work Becomes Home and Home Becomes Work by Arlie Russell Hochschild (New York: Owl Books, Reissued 2001). Exposes negative cycle to American trend toward excessive work hours. When parents work too many hours, it creates stress at home, which in turn leads parents to spend more time at work to avoid stress at home. Discusses alternatives and solutions to this dilemma.

Timeshifting: Creating More Time to Enjoy Your Life by Stephan Rechtschaffen MD (New York: Doubleday, 1997). Physician/author focuses on how we respond to a faced-paced environment by aligning our own rhythms to that pace and how we can break that reaction to restore a sense of abundant time in our lives.

MISCELLANEOUS

Take Back Your Time Day [www.timeday.org]. This web site is the focal point for the campaign planned for the fall of 2003 called Take Back Your Time. The first Take Back Your Time Day is scheduled for October 24, 2003, at which time thousands of people across the United States and in other countries will work fewer hours or not at all. The purpose of this national initiative is to build awareness and to open dialogue about the issues related to excessive work hours.

NOTE: *Additions and updates to these resources can be found on The Simplicity Resource Guide at www.gallagherpress.com/pierce.*

LESSON 6

WORKING WITH PASSION

SIMPLICITY IS NOT AN ANTI-WORK MOVEMENT

Fifty years ago, the typical North American family consisted of one wage earner (usually the husband), one homemaker (usually the wife), and several children. Gradually women decided—with the support of the women's liberation movement—that they, too, wanted the economic power, intellectual stimulation, and camaraderie provided by work. It became culturally acceptable for women to have children and a career simultaneously, and indeed they did. Today, in 64 percent of U.S. families with children, both parents work.[1] Women have made substantial inroads into male domains—high-level corporate management and prominence in professions such as law and medicine.

How does the simplicity movement's message to work less fit into this picture? Simplicity may appear, on the surface, to devalue work and the rights that women fought so hard to obtain. In fact, some people view simplicity as an anti-work movement. They mistakenly associate living simply with working as little as possible, conjuring up the image of an economically-challenged person sitting in a coffee house sipping lattes, contemplating life, and maybe dashing off a poem or two.

While this sounds like a lovely way to spend an afternoon, it is not a common lifestyle among people who live simply. Most are ordinary people who work for a living, live in urban or suburban areas, and actively enjoy friends and family. For the most part, they are not mainstream drop-outs.[2] Purposeful work, even for those who are financially independent, is important to the vast majority of people who live simply.

Simplicity's message then is not to give up work but rather to balance it with the rest of life. What started out as a quality of life choice for women—the opportunity to work—is now seen as an economic necessity. Unfortunately, however, it is nearly impossible for a family of two full-time working parents with children to live a quality, balanced life. Twenty-four hours in a day is simply not enough to work well, parent well, and have enough left over for an inner life, community, and leisure.

This doesn't mean that women should quit their jobs and go back to being full-time mothers and homemakers. But it may mean that both men and women need to devote less time to work if work/life balance is desired. In other words, we must work less, want less, and spend less.

A NEW DEFINITION OF WORK

Nothing contributes so much to tranquilize the mind as a steady purpose—a point on which the soul may fix its intellectual eye.

Mary Shelley

Discussing the subject of work is problematic because we don't share a common definition of it. Webster's dictionary defines it as "physical or mental effort exerted to do or make something." This definition would include almost all activity during our waking hours, from brushing our teeth to running a billion-dollar company. In the context of simplicity, we can define work as purposeful activity that (1) uses a person's talents and skills, (2) to make a contribution to the world—for the welfare of others or the earth, (3) in a manner that is in harmony with the worker's values, and (4) is in balance with the rest of the person's life. Whether an activity generates compensation or social recognition is not material to the true essence of work.

Most of us work to earn a living but, based on this broader definition, activities such as parenting, maintaining a home, creating objects of art, and volunteering in the community would all qualify as work. Also, activities that develop knowledge or skills in preparation for work, such as college education or vocational training, should be considered work.

Most of us engage in several forms of work. For example, our work might include parenting, a traditional job, and volunteering in the community. Or a college student might work at his college courses plus have a part-time job.

North American culture tends to value only work that produces an income, with volunteer work receiving minimal secondary recognition. Rarely is parenting children, caring for an elderly parent, producing art (unless it is paid for), or leading a Boy Scout troop considered work. These activities are certainly not included in the gross national product. But in fact, they are as important to society as any traditional job that pays a salary.

If we are fortunate, our life's work can be delightfully close to play. It can be difficult to distinguish the two. This may explain why many of the participants in my simplicity study, most of whom enjoy their work, are not too concerned with saving for retirement. In general, they desire and expect to continue working through their retirement years. This may or may not be realistic or financially prudent, but it is notable that many are not counting the days to retirement.

A good way to determine if your work is also a form of play is to ask yourself this question: Would you continue working if you won the lottery or inherited a bundle from a distant relative? If you love your work so much you'd do it for free, it's undoubtedly also a form of play. When I ask people if they would continue their work if they no longer had to earn a living, most say they would *not* continue with their current job, but would do other work. One of the goals in living simply is to engage in work you would continue doing even if you received an unexpected financial windfall.

It is not hard work that is dreary; it is superficial work.

Edith Hamilton

PURPOSE AND FULFILLMENT IN WORK

What about the intangible aspects of work? What do we seek in work beyond the monetary rewards? For one, we seem to be intrinsically wired to test ourselves, to stretch and grow, to develop whatever talents and skills we have, to make a contribution. In *The Reinvention of Work*, Matthew Fox explains that working tells us we are needed in the universe, that we have a home in the universe. Without it, we are "cosmically homeless."

Work gives us a sense of purpose in life, or rather many purposes. When we work, we know that our efforts and our lives have meaning beyond keeping our bodies alive as long as possible. Even if our work is not particularly fulfilling, we are still making an impact, if only a tiny ripple on the ocean of life. This is one reason why it is valuable for people in the later stages of life to continue to work, if only as a volunteer for a few hours a week.

Work typically has several purposes: (1) it may provide income for you and your family to live on, (2) it may produce valuable goods or services needed by others, and (3) it may give you a sense of personal fulfillment. Many people focus on the first purpose primarily, to a lesser degree on the second purpose, and only coincidentally on the third purpose. In contrast, people who live simply generally assign the third purpose—personal fulfillment—as much importance as the other two. In fact, it is so important that they will downsize their living expenses, if necessary, in exchange for fulfilling work even if that work pays less. They simply are not willing to work in unsatisfying jobs just to fund the *good life* as defined by corporate advertisers, their neighbors, families or friends.

Clearly, work that serves all three purposes (unless you don't need the income to meet your needs), is ideal. Unfortunately, it's not always possible. Some people engage in one type of work to earn money and seek personal fulfillment in other work. A classic example is the artist who waits tables part-time to support himself so he can devote time and energy to his art.

The more a soul conforms to the sanity of others, the more does it become insane.

Mary Webb

Personal fulfillment can be a function of how mindful we are in our work. If we focus on our interactions with others and the various tasks we perform, rather than on how boring, stressful, or unsatisfying those tasks appear to be, we may discover a whole new job waiting for us.

The work we do to create inner simplicity (see Lesson 8) produces a sense of inner peace and happiness. If our happiness is centered within, we are less likely to be disappointed if our work environment is not totally perfect. Expectations reduce joy. If you live without expectations that certain results will occur, you will rarely be disappointed. To the extent we can live without expectations, we open ourselves to unexpected highs.

AUTHENTIC WORK

To experience personal fulfillment, your work must be authentic—you must feel at home with your work, and it must allow you to be who you truly are. If your work requires you to play roles that feel artificial to you or to dress in ways that feel uncomfortable, it's not authentic for you. Authentic work produces a feeling of intrinsic satisfaction because it allows you to develop and apply *your* unique talents, skills, and interests. It is often expressed in the comment: "This work just feels right for me."

If your work is not authentic, you are likely to feel like an imposter. If you choose work primarily for its income potential, or its high status, or because your family expects you to go into a particular line of work, or because it was the first job offered to you after school, or because you haven't a clue about what work would be your most authentic expression, or because you have done this work for so many years and are afraid of starting over, or for any reason other than your desire for personally fulfilling work, you are selling yourself short. You are also short-changing society, which gets the most value from people who are passionate in their work.

Yes, it can be challenging to find work that offers you both personal fulfillment and an adequate income. But I've seen too many people do it to doubt that it's possible. It may require an adjustment in living expenses, although not necessarily. It may take time—typically anywhere from six months to two years—to make the changes necessary to allow you to do this work. It likely will take courage, patience, and persistence as well. But it can be done, and I would bet a night out on the town that whatever you give up materially—if that's what it takes—will have less value to you than personally fulfilling work.

Let's dare to be ourselves, for we do that better than anyone else can.

Shirley Briggs

Finding your authentic work is complicated by the fact that in North America we are taught to view work as a measure of self-worth, as a form of social standing and status. I suspect this cultural belief played a role in the results of a 1994 RAND study of California attorneys.[3] Half said they would not go into the law if they had it to do over again. As relatively high-income earners, attorneys have more opportunities than most to downscale and still enjoy a moderate standard of living. (As one who walked away from a law practice and never looked back, I can report that there is life after the law.)

It's possible that a law career was not an authentic choice to begin with for some of the attorneys in the study. How many young people choose careers because of the lure of money and status, only to discover they don't genuinely enjoy the required day-to-day activities? And how can young people determine what they are genuinely interested in when society teaches them that wealth and status are the most important values in life?

It may also be that these dissatisfied attorneys, like me, enjoyed their work for a number of years but later decided it was too much—too much stress, too much encroachment on personal time, too deficient in civility. And the same or similar things could be said by others at some point in their careers. For whatever reasons, sometimes we discover we have lost the juice, the passion, for our work. By then, however, we may feel trapped, perhaps because we've developed a certain standard of living and have mistaken it for the *good life*.

This is not to say that if we reach this place in our work, we should necessarily quit our jobs and seek other careers. Some of us just need to go through a process of re-examination and rejuvenation to restore the passion we once had for our work. For others, doing the same work in a different setting is the answer. For example, a corporate attorney might work in the field of environmental law, or a physician might work in a clinic serving the poor.

Uncertainty is the prerequisite to gaining knowledge and frequently the result as well.

Edith Hamilton

Taking time off, either in reduced work hours or possibly a sabbatical, can be very helpful in this regard. Reading relevant books—such as *Transforming Practices* by Steven Keeva for the legal profession—will stimulate your thoughts about what's best for you.

Fifty or sixty years ago, you typically worked in one career your entire life, sometimes with just one company. Today, we have a lot more choices. We can change jobs or careers—even start all over with education—without being considered unstable ne'er-do-wells. Still, there are risks involved. You may find that a new work choice is no more satisfying than the previous one, but for different reasons. You may have to put yourself out there in the world as a beginner in a new field, capable of being rejected or judged harshly. You may lose the security of a higher income and status in the community. You and your family may find the required adjustments to be extremely difficult at first. However, I've yet to meet someone who left unfulfilling work for the promise of more satisfying work and later regretted it.

Living simply serves us in the quest for work that satisfies. To the extent we are not wedded to a highly materialistic lifestyle, we have more economic freedom in our work choices. To the extent that we have learned to separate quality of life from standard of living, we are more likely to discover our authentic work.

DISCOVERING YOUR PASSION

At one point not too long ago, after reading one too many self-help books, I decided to create success in my work through the common practice of affirmations. I started a daily practice of saying to myself, "It is my intention and desire to be wildly successful in the field of simplicity." After doing this for a while, I questioned myself about why I wanted this success. Was it money? Was it professional recognition? Nothing seemed to fit. Neither of these things, while nice to have, seemed to motivate me. (I would never have quit the practice of law if money and recognition were my top priorities.)

Intuition is a spiritual faculty and does not explain, but simply points the way.

Florence Scovel Shinn

I finally realized that the feeling of success fuels my passion for work. It keeps me excited. When indications of success come my way, it makes me want to do more, it gives me hope for our world, and the passion for my work grows. This is true whether the success comes from readers who say that my book, *Choosing Simplicity*, changed their lives or as a lucrative speaking offer.

I have since changed my daily affirmation to say, "It is my intention and desire to feel passion in my work and to make a contribution to the world." If I can feel these things, then I am successful. Of course, I also need to earn some income; my husband and I are not financially independent. But it's been my experience that if I focus on doing authentic work, money is there when we need it.

But how do we find our passion in work? In many different, unique ways. For me, I read an article on voluntary simplicity in September of 1995 and knew at once I wanted to work in this field. While much had already been done in the field of simplicity, I could see that there were new roads to travel, new paths to explore. It was and continues to be very exciting for me.

I believe we have considerable intuitive knowledge about what work would be authentic choices for us. The challenge is to remove the inner clutter so you can hear what you already know to be true. Again, the work you do to develop inner simplicity (see Lesson 8) will serve you well in this area. Reading, thinking, and talking it over with friends and family are all tools that can help you discover your passion. The Recommended Resources at the end of this lesson will get you started.

WORK/LIFE BALANCE

As I've noted before, work ideally is in balance with the rest of life. But what about the person who works 60 hours a week, is passionate about her work, and also loves the life of luxury that her earning power gives her? What's wrong with that lifestyle? Maybe nothing, but for most of us, plenty. Such a lifestyle needs close examination. For example, does it pass the *spouse/significant other* test? What does the passionate workaholic say to her spouse or significant other at the end of the day? Does she share tales of satisfaction and fulfillment, or does she relate stories of stress and frustration? Is she passionate about the specific tasks that make up her work, or is she more attached to the prestige and salary of her position?

Work and leisure are complementary parts of the same process. They cannot be separated without destroying the joy of work and the bliss of leisure.

E.F. Schumacher

How much of what we call passion for our work is really an addiction to the stimulation and pressure inherent in our jobs? Workaholism is similar to other addictions. We become addicted to the adrenaline that constant work provides. Like other addictions, we may be in denial. If we believe that we absolutely need a certain level of income to live happily, and that it is improbable to find other, more satisfying work to produce that income, might we tell ourselves we really love our work because it is too frightening to consider the prospect of material insecurity or unhappiness?

If you work 60 hours a week, you will have little time or energy to devote to relationships, a spiritual life, connection with nature, and good health practices, all of which contribute to a high quality of life. Perhaps if you are one of those rare individuals who need little sleep—like my husband who feels refreshed after five hours of sleep—you could live a balanced life with a heavy work schedule. But I am doubtful. (I've tried to persuade my husband he should do all the housework because he has more waking hours at his disposal, but so far, I have failed miserably in this attempt.)

When your work is your life, you become one-dimensional. You are less developed as a human being and consequently have less to offer the world. Moreover, you are at risk of losing your sense of self should something happen to prevent you from working. If you burn yourself out and eventually retire completely while still physically healthy, you are likely to feel bored and anxious.

A friend recently told me about two very successful publishers. As a couple, they shared a passion for books. Upon retiring in the evening, they each brought a huge pile of manuscripts to bed with them. Their bedroom, which they shared, was furnished with his and hers queen-sized beds. Both claimed they loved their work. After the children were grown, however, they went their separate ways, realizing they had lived parallel lives, with neither one ever knowing much about the other except for what they did in their profession.

Ok, let's assume you're sold on living a balanced life. But you still have that job and that boss who expects you to produce at a level that requires excessive work hours. What can you do? If you enjoy your work other than its long hours, you might first explore alternatives with your employer, who may be more flexible than you expect.

For workaholics, all the eggs of self-esteem are in the basket of work.

Judith M. Bardwick

You might consider job sharing, telecommuting, or a reduced work schedule. When you approach your employer, you should come armed with a proposal on how your employer's objectives can also be met. If you are a talented, valued employee, your employer will be more amenable to consider your proposal rather than risk replacing you with an unknown prospect. If you are not viewed as a talented, valued employee—either because you lack skill for this particular work, or your employer is a misguided fool—you are probably in the wrong job and should consider a change.

I've heard many success stories of people who persuaded their employers to allow them to work in unusual ways. Sometimes people resign their employee status but continue working for their former employer as a consultant, often earning the same or a greater amount, for fewer hours of work. I encourage you to explore whatever options would work for you. You might be very surprised by what you can negotiate.

WORKING FOR YOURSELF

In the United States, 12 million people, out of a total labor force of 142 million, are self-employed. Incidentally, this represents a 20 percent increase in self-employment during the last two years. About half of the self-employed work at home.[4] My guess is that this trend will continue unless businesses become much more savvy at creating jobs that permit work/life balance.

Self-employment offers you greater freedom and control over your work—from work hours and dress code to quality control of the services or goods you provide. The downsides include greater fluctuations in income and possibly the loss of camaraderie experienced in a group work setting. It is questionable whether self-employment offers less overall financial security than working for others, however. In fact, it may provide more security, especially if you produce goods or services that are in demand. You cannot get laid off or fired if you work for yourself. If you work at home, your ancillary costs of working—commuting, wardrobe, restaurant lunches—will be eliminated or reduced substantially.

If you risk nothing, then you risk everything.

Geena Davis

Self-employment typically offers considerable variety, allowing you to develop more skills than you thought possible. One simplicity study participant, an owner of a carpet cleaning business, explains:

> As an entrepreneur, you get to wear many hats: production, marketing, public relations, accountant, repair person, purchaser, janitor, etc. With such a range of tasks, it's hard to get bored, and even possible to get smarter.

Of course, self-employment is not for everyone. Some people need the structure and enjoy the team environment provided by many traditional jobs. Others do not feel comfortable with the income fluctuations inherent in working for yourself. If you live in the United States and want health insurance, you will need to obtain an individual or family policy. You may be able to obtain coverage as a member of a trade or professional association. As discussed in Lesson 3, this is an extra cost of living to be considered in your total financial picture and not by itself a good reason to reject self-employment.

In *Making a Living Without a Job*, Barbara Winter advocates being "joyfully jobless" by creating multiple profit centers as a self-employed person. The idea is to develop several sources of income or side businesses rather than rely on just one. Sometimes they relate to each other, sometimes not. For example, I earn my living in three major areas: writing books, public speaking and workshops, and writing freelance articles for magazines. Each of these activities relates to and supports the other two. Another person might work part-time as an accountant and teach piano lessons on the side.

This approach offers variety and an opportunity to develop and use your diverse talents and skills. It also provides greater financial security because if one source of income falls away, you can rely on others while you develop one or more profit centers. Working in this manner also allows you to maintain independence and autonomy in your work. This priority is reflected in the comments of one simplicity study participant: "Multiple income sources seem to be what keeps me afloat without selling my soul. I am determined to work locally and at things I believe in."

A ship in port is safe, but that's not what ships are built for.

Grace Murray Hopper

If self-employment appeals to you, then living simply—reducing your monetary requirements to only what you need or cherish—will give you more financial flexibility to create your dream job.

A WORK-FRIENDLY SOCIETY

In Lesson 5, we considered the time benefits of reduced work hours to the employee and possible ways to mitigate productivity losses for the employer. In this lesson, we will examine the broader benefits of social and public policies that favor work/life balance.

Apart from reduced work hours, work hour flexibility is very helpful in meeting parenting and elder care needs. Some companies offer a certain number of *flex hours* to use when needed. To the extent that we, as a society, can facilitate families meeting these needs directly, there will be less of a burden on society in general, not to mention the advantages of having family members care for each other.

In addition to legislating a reduced work-hour week, we could, as a society, establish other financial incentives, in the form of tax credits, subsidies, or payroll tax adjustments, to induce employers to reduce work hours and offer other programs to support employee work/life balance. Taxpayers would be making a good investment in providing these incentives, because work hour reductions and flexibility allow people to tend to their families and their health. The social benefits of such policies would likely include stronger families and communities, reduced crime, and less substance abuse.

As Anders Hayden explains in his book, *Sharing the Work, Sparing the Planet*, reducing work hours can have a substantial positive impact on unemployment. Traditionally, we have dealt with unemployment by increasing economic growth, which in turn produces more jobs. However, the earth is on a crash course with consumption, and it cannot absorb unlimited material output, the likely result of continual economic growth. Furthermore, as productivity and efficiency increase through improved technology, the need for certain types of labor decreases. By reducing work hours, we employ a greater number of people *and* offer them a higher quality of life. This is in contrast to the current approach of creating artificial needs for increased materialism in order to create more jobs.

In a society that judges self-worth on productivity, it's no wonder we fall pray to the misconception that the more we do, the more we're worth.

Ellen Sue Stern

Reducing work hours has been a key contributor to increased levels of employment in a number of countries, including West Germany (43 percent of all full-time jobs created from 1983-1992) and the Netherlands (unemployment reduced from 12 percent in 1983 to 3.4 percent in 1999).[5] There is no reason why this couldn't be effective in North America.

Employment practices that support work/life balance will develop in time if workers demand it. What we need is a cultural revolution in which we acknowledge the importance of work, but not at the expense of other vital aspects of life, such as family, community, spirituality, and leisure. To the extent that you take steps that value work/life balance in your own life and in the lives of your family, friends, colleagues, and employees (should you be an employer), you contribute to this evolving social transformation.

CONCLUSION

Work is essential to life. We must work to sustain our bodies and nourish our minds and spirits. But in North America, we have elevated working and spending to the level of worship, causing considerable damage to ourselves and the earth.

We have doubled our economic productivity in the last 50 years. We had a choice: we could have halved our work hours if we were willing to accept the standard of living we enjoyed in the 1950's.[6] Instead we chose to triple our consumption levels, which required families to work twice as hard to pay for the increased spending. Somewhere there is a middle ground.

LESSON ASSIGNMENTS

Life shrinks or expands in proportion to one's courage.

Anais Nin

FROM YOUR PERSONAL VIEWPOINT . . .

1. Write down all the forms of work that you do, whether in or outside the home, for compensation, for your own personal satisfaction, or as a volunteer. Estimate the approximate number of weekly hours devoted to each type of work.
2. What value does society place on each type of work you do?
3. What value do you place on the work you do? What purposes (other than earning money) does your work serve for you personally?
4. On a scale of 1 to 5 (with 5 being the highest), how much meaning and fulfillment do you receive from each type of work that you do?
5. On a scale of 1 to 5 (with 5 being the highest), how much passion do you feel for your work?
6. If you inherited large sums of money, would you continue to do any of the work that you are doing today? If not, what would you do instead?
7. What possibilities are there for you to find more meaning and fulfillment in your current work?
8. What possibilities are there for you to replace less meaningful work with more fulfilling work?
9. What type of work would you like to be doing in three to five years?
10. Does your current work support work/life balance in your life? Describe how it does or does not. If not, what

changes could you make to establish that balance? Would it require a change in jobs or careers or adjustments in your current job or career?

LOOKING AT THE BIGGER PICTURE . . .

11. How would you describe the work culture in your country? For example, what values are emphasized—productivity, high quality products or services, profits, employee recognition, fair wages, work/life balance? What are the strengths and weaknesses of the work culture in your country?
12. Think of people you know who seem to have passion for their work and who keep their work in balance with the rest of their lives. What are the critical factors that allow them to work in this way? What changes would society need to make to allow most people to work this way?

I don't want to get to the end of my life and find that I lived just the length of it. I want to have lived the width of it as well.

Diane Ackerman

LIFEWORK ASSIGNMENTS

1. Practice working with greater mindfulness. Each time you return from a break during your work hours, take a deep breath and think about bringing a sense of calm and stillness into your work, even if your work is noisy, hectic or otherwise crazy-making. It can also be helpful to take a deep breath each time the phone rings before picking it up to greet the caller.
2. If you have negative or mixed feelings about your current work, start a practice of writing in a journal daily about your work day. Write down exactly what was satisfying and what was stressful or frustrating. Over time, you will get a clearer picture of how close your current work meets your needs—whether it is an authentic choice for you.
3. Consider your work goals for three to five years down the road. Map out a plan of how you might get from here to there. If your ideal work would produce less income, how can you reduce your expenses to make your work dream come true? If you need to develop new skills and knowledge for your ideal job, how can you do that gradually over time without overextending yourself?

ANNUAL CHECK-UP

1. Review and answer the first 10 questions in the lesson assignments above as they apply to your work life now, one year later. Are there any significant changes in your responses from a year ago?
2. What are your work-related goals for the coming year in terms of doing authentic work that is in balance with the rest of your life?
3. Review the lifework assignments above and decide if you want to take on one or more of these tasks.

Nature doesn't move in a straight line, and as part of nature, neither do we.

Gloria Steinem

RECOMMENDED RESOURCES

BOOKS

Do What You Love, The Money Will Follow: Discovering Your Right Livelihood by Marsha Sinetar (New York: Bantam Doubleday Dell, Reissued 1989). An inspirational best seller, the author contends that it is possible to do work that you enjoy while also providing for your material needs. Explores concept of right livelihood and describes various paths people have taken to experience it.

Downshifting: How to Work Less and Enjoy Life More by John D. Drake (San Francisco: Berrett-Koehler, 2001). Psychologist and former CEO of large human resources consulting firm discusses negative impact of excessive work hours and offers practical advice on how to downsize. Reviews options such as flextime schedules, gradual retirement plans, and requesting a lower level job within the same organization.

Follow Your Bliss by Hal Zina Bennett and Susan J. Sparrow (Upper Lake, CA: Tenacity Press, 1997). Authors show how to first discover, and then follow, your bliss through exploration of your inner self. With this self-knowledge, you can then embark on your life paths, creating work and relationships that bring inner peace and fulfillment.

How to Find the Work You Love by Laurence G. Boldt (New York: Arkana, 1996). Guides the reader to discover his *calling* in life. Offers suggestions to achieve that result, emphasizing four elements—integrity, service, enjoyment, and excellence.

The Joy of Not Working: A Book for the Retired, Unemployed, and Overworked by Ernie Zelinski (Berkeley, CA: Ten Speed Pr, 3rd edition, 1997). Explores the positive values of leisure time and activities. Examines the difficult challenges of embracing leisure joyfully in a culture that celebrates workaholism.

Making a Living Without a Job: Winning Ways for Creating Work that You Love by Barbara J. Winter (New York: Bantam Doubleday Dell, 1993). Advocates self-employment, sometimes in multiple services or businesses, as an alternative to a salaried position working for others. Offers guidance and encouragement to those who want to combine their passions with income-producing activities.

The Man Who Mistook His Job for a Life: A Chronic Overachiever Finds the Way Home by Jonathon Lazear (New York: Crown Publishers, 2001). Memoir of a workaholic. Explores inner journey of a man whose self-worth was defined primarily by what he did for a living to a person who broadened his world and identity to include a full human experience.

The Overworked American: The Unexpected Decline of Leisure by Juliet B. Schor (New York: BasicBooks, Reprinted 1993). Discusses the evolution of American culture of work and consumerism, the work-and-spend treadmill. Charts the loss of leisure in America and offers compelling arguments for restructuring our work to provide more time for living.

The Reinvention of Work: A New Vision of Livelihood for Our Time by Matthew Fox (New York: Harper San Francisco, 1995). Radical priest proposes a spirituality of work that allows people to experience a revitalization of daily work, a world where the self is not sacrificed for a job but is sanctified by authentic *soul work*. Promotes a harmonious integration of personal and professional lives.

Simplify Your Work Life: Ways to Change the Way You Work So You Have More Time to Live by Elaine St. James (New York: Hyperion, 2001). Offers practical tips for managing work life, including topics such as setting boundaries between work and home, work relationships, and productivity.

The Stirring of the Soul in the Workplace by Alan Briskin (San Francisco: Berrett-Koehler, Reprinted 1998). Business consultant examines how organizational structures interfere with the experience of the *soul* in the workplace—passion, creativity, imagination, caring, and meaning—and reflects on how we might integrate the whole human being into the workplace.

Transforming Practices: Finding Joy and Satisfaction in the Legal Life by Steven Keeva (Chicago: McGraw Hill/Contemporary Books, 1999). Author examines the spiritual crisis in the legal profession and offers advice and inspiration to lawyers who want to return to the ideals they had when they graduated from law school.

Un-Jobbing: The Adult Liberation Handbook by Michael Fogler (Lexington, KY: Free Choice Press, 2nd edition, 1999). Freelance musician and peace activist discusses the benefits of living a home-based, freelance-work lifestyle rather than work in a single, full-time, career-oriented job.

Vacation Work's International Directory of Voluntary Work by Louise Whetter and Victoria Pybus (Oxford: Vacation Work, 7th Ed, 2000). Lists over 700 organizations throughout the world that offer volunteer work opportunities. Some provide stipends for room and board, travel expenses, or other compensation.

When Work Doesn't Work Anymore: Women, Work, and Identity by Elizabeth Perle McKenna (New York: Bantam Doubleday Dell, 1998). Part memoir, part social essay, this former publisher focuses on the successful career woman who has integrated the traditional male definition of success, experienced it, and then concludes it doesn't work. Solutions from women interviewed by the author point to many examples of living more simply.

Work to Live: The Guide to Getting a Life by Joe Robinson (New York: Perigee, 2003). Founder of Work to Live Campaign [www.worktolive.info] criticizes American practice of excessive work hours and offers suggestions for breaking out of the burnout trap, getting more vacation time, and working fewer hours.

Working from Home: Everything You Need to Know about Living and Working under the Same Roof by Paul Edwards and Sarah Edwards (New York: J.P. Tarcher, 5th edition, 1999). Comprehensive manual for starting and maintaining a home-based business, including advice on computers, staying out of debt, and maintaining balance between work and your personal life.

MISCELLANEOUS

Changing Course [www.changingcourse.com] offers a free newsletter and other resources to help people discover and follow their dreams of a more fulfilling work/life doing what they love. Offers ideas on creative alternatives to traditional jobs.

Take Back Your Time Day [www.timeday.org]. This web site is the focal point for the campaign planned for the fall of 2003 called Take Back Your Time. The first Take Back Your Time Day is scheduled for October 24, 2003, on which day thousands of people across the United States and in some other countries will work fewer hours or not at all. The purpose of this national initiative is to build awareness and to open dialogue about the issues related to excessive work hours.

NOTE: *Additions and updates to these resources can be found on The Simplicity Resource Guide at www.gallagherpress.com/pierce.*

LESSON 7

Moving About at Home and Abroad

IT'S ALL IN THE JOURNEY

For the most part, transporting ourselves from point A to point B is a bothersome but necessary chore. It's just a part of life, we tell ourselves. Typically, we aim to get to our destination in the least amount of time and with the least amount of fuss as possible. When driving becomes routine, we switch to automatic pilot mode—our car seems to know the way to work without any mental effort on our part. One conversation *not* heard at the office water cooler is a glowing description of the drive to work.

The time we spend transporting ourselves and our children to work, school, stores, social activities, and recreational destinations can add up to a significant number of hours each week. For that reason alone, the journey itself should offer its own rewards or, at a minimum, it should be a conscious experience!

Obviously, the way we travel—whether it's cross town, cross country, or to a foreign destination—affects the quality of our transportation experience. Due to the growth of urban sprawl and suburban isolation in America, we use automobiles for 82 percent of our trips while the Germans, French, and British all use cars for less than half their trips.[1] Approximately 30 percent of all trips in the Netherlands and in Copenhagen, Denmark, are by bicycle compared to one percent in the United States.[2] The time spent sitting in traffic jams in the larger U.S. cities has increased from an average of 11 hours per person annually in 1982 to 36 hours in 1999, with Los Angeles coming in the highest at 56 hours per year.[3]

A fundamental component of simplicity is experiencing life directly with our hearts, minds, and bodies. If our primary mode of transportation is the automobile, we spend a great deal of time in a machine. In a car, we are one step removed from life. We don't breathe fresh air. Our feet do not touch the ground. Driving along at 30 to 60 miles an hour, we can only glance superficially at our surroundings. We are unlikely to stop the car to have a spontaneous chat with a friend or neighbor. Our capacity to experience life directly is diminished.

Using public transportation has similar drawbacks. However, riding trains and buses has the advantage of freeing us from the mental concentration required of driving, not to mention the substantial savings of the earth's resources that results from transporting groups of people together.

Of course, automobile transportation also has advantages. The obvious one is that you can travel greater distances in less time than walking or bicycling, for example. And driving through beautiful countryside is a pleasure all its own. But for most of us, the time we spend in moving vehicles is not something we would do for its own sake. Moreover, a city that is heavily dependent on the automobile produces congestion and pollution for everyone, pedestrians and automobile drivers alike.

The true traveler is he who goes on foot, and even then, he sits down a lot of the time.

Colette

WALKING AND BICYCLING

People who live simply often structure their lives to minimize the use of automobiles. Thirty-six percent of the two-adult families in my simplicity study either share a car or live without one. They favor walking and bicycling for the benefit of the earth, their budgets, and their arteries. Combining a short walk (less than one mile) with public transportation is often a viable choice. One woman, whose primary source of transportation is a secondhand bicycle, talks about the freedom of living without a car:

> For many people I know, having a car seems closely intertwined with their sense of freedom—freedom to go where they want, at any time they want. In my life it's the opposite. I feel free without a car—free from car payments, maintenance, and traffic tickets. And I have the freedom to park my bicycle practically anywhere!

Walking and bicycling can be quite pleasurable in themselves. We experience our natural environment more directly. We see so much more than when driving. Try walking a route you normally drive. You are likely to see many things you never saw before—a gorgeous oak tree, a charming fence, or interesting architecture. The exercise of walking or bicycling also releases endorphins in your body, giving you a sense of well-being.

Poets and writers over the centuries have extolled the creative benefits of walking. I have experienced this many times myself. When I walk, new ideas pop into my mind as if by magic, without any effort on my part. It's as if the earth is delighted to have my company and responds by offering these gifts.

Our reluctance to consider walking and bicycling is often related to time deprivation—the feeling that there just aren't enough hours in a day. However, if we reduce our work hours for all the reasons discussed in Lesson 5, and if we also choose the location of our home and work carefully, walking and bicycling can be realistic options. Because I live simply and only work 25 to 30 hours per week, I have the time to walk to town (30 minutes each way) several times a week. I get good exercise, do my errands, and feel a spiritual lift from walking through the beautiful forested town I live in.

"Normal" is getting dressed in clothes that you buy for work, driving through traffic in a car that you are still paying for, in order to get to the job that you need so you can pay for the clothes, car, and the house that you leave empty all day in order to afford to live in it.

Ellen Goodman

Other benefits of walking and bicycling include increased mobility for certain segments of the population—children, the elderly who no longer drive, and low income people who cannot afford a car. Obviously, walking and bicycling offer improved health for everyone. The lack of exercise resulting from increasing dependence on the automobile has contributed substantially to an obesity crisis in the world, now estimated to affect 1.1 billion people.[4] If we walk or bicycle to transport ourselves, we serve two needs at the same time—transportation and good health.

Walking or bicycling is a win-win-win proposition: it preserves the earth's resources, enhances our physical and mental health, and reduces our cost of living.

EXPLORING ALTERNATIVES

A major challenge to using earth-friendly transportation relates to the sheer distances we travel. So many of us live in suburbs and must commute 20, 30, or more miles to work (sometimes *many* more miles). Perhaps we should consider a new approach to integrating the different parts of our lives. For most of us, our choice of work is paramount. Once work is selected, we choose a home that best meets our needs. And finally, we decide which transportation options will support our work and home choices. The relative importance of each of these factors is illustrated in Figure 1-A.

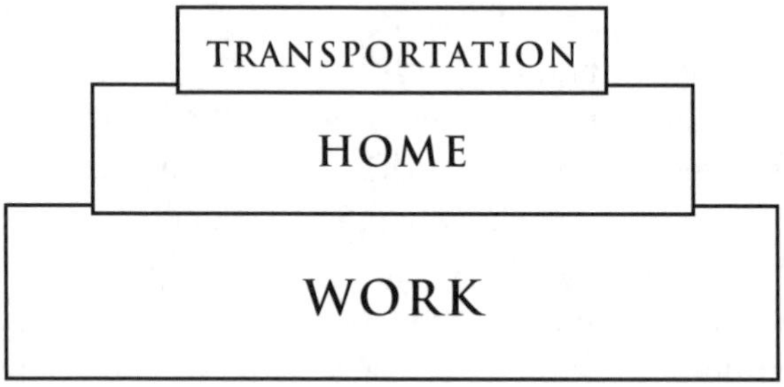

Figure 1-A

Neglecting small things because one wishes to do great things is the excuse of the faint-hearted.

Alexandra David-Neel

Another approach is to view these three elements—work, housing, and transportation—as equally valued sides of a triangle (see Figure 1-B). Each element must support the other two. For example, if we want to avoid long commutes to work, we might decide to trade our large home in the suburbs for a similarly priced, smaller home in town, or for a home that is closer to work. Or we might decide to give up a particular job opportunity with a long commute in order to reclaim those long hours we'd spend commuting. With gasoline prices on the rise, living closer to our workplace becomes an increasingly important economic factor. Or we may decide to reduce our work hours to free up time to walk or bicycle to work and other destinations.

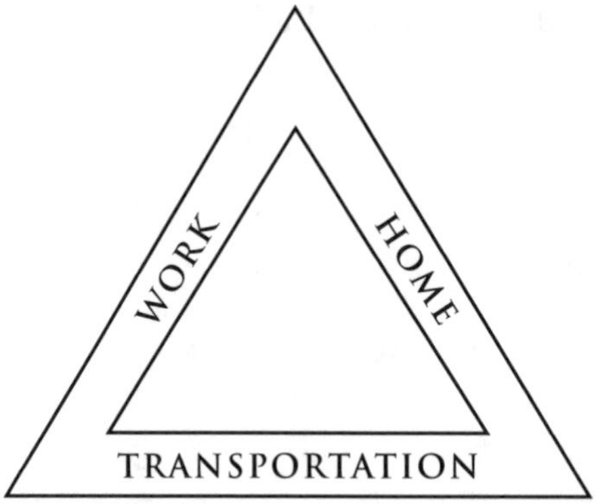

Figure 1-B

This approach requires a different mindset. Instead of favoring work as the most important decision in our lives, we focus instead on the entire lifestyle package. To the extent that we can live in livable neighborhoods, towns, and cities (see Lesson 5 for a discussion of this trend), we will have greater opportunities to integrate these basic infrastructure elements.

ENVIRONMENTAL CONSIDERATIONS

Clearly, the automobile is a poor choice for transportation from an environmental point of view. For starters, construction of an automobile requires one to two tons of raw materials, while a bicycle typically weighs only 28 pounds or so.[5] The negative environmental impact of carbon-dioxide emissions from automobiles is well-documented. Automobiles using alternative energy sources, such as a hybrid car that uses a combination of gasoline and electricity and the hydrogen fuel cell car, are being developed to ameliorate the damage to the earth.

People on horses look better than they are. People in cars look worse than they are.

Marya Mannes

But we don't need to wait for these technologies to lessen our impact on the earth. There are other ways we can reduce our dependence on the automobile. For example, reducing the distance between your home and work is often more effective than driving a car that gets a high level of miles per gallon. Driving a hybrid car 40 miles a day will do more harm to the earth than driving a car with poor gas mileage five miles a day. In the lesson assignments below, you will be asked to calculate your estimated annual gasoline usage.

Many transportation alternatives are available for residents of cities and livable towns, including walking, bicycling, using low-impact powered vehicles such as electric scooters or bicycles, and public transportation. Some people are able to use these alternatives as their primary sources of transportation and will rent a car for the occasional trip out of town.

Each time you use one of these transportation alternatives, or share a car ride with one or more people, you reduce your impact on the earth compared to driving solo in an automobile. Of course, while walking and bicycling are the best choices to preserve the earth's resources, it's quite a challenge to structure your life to use these alternatives in car-dependent North

America. We can't do it alone. We need to implement earth-friendly social and public policies to make the required changes.

HOW SOCIAL AND PUBLIC POLICIES CAN HELP

There are many approaches to creating earth-friendly transportation alternatives, including taxing negative choices, subsidizing positive alternatives, implementing carpooling and car sharing programs, and creating livable towns and cities.

No enemy action had silenced the rebirth of new life in this stricken world. The people had done it themselves.

Rachel Carson

One obvious option would be to tax gasoline to reflect the true cost of its damage to the environment. However, without viable alternatives, this would place a heavy burden on commuters. On the other hand, if such taxes were implemented gradually over a period of time, perhaps 10 years, this would soften the burden and give individuals and communities time to explore alternative means of transportation. Using gasoline tax proceeds to subsidize public transportation would provide economic incentives for people to use their cars less and public transportation more, which in turn would produce revenues to develop better public transportation.

A graduated gasoline tax policy would also allow people time to find work and places to live that are closer together. Indeed, it might result in rehabilitating our cities, creating more livable neighborhoods. It could also provide incentives to turn our suburbs into livable communities with more opportunities to live, work, and play within a smaller radius than is the norm today.

Likewise, we could restructure car insurance costs and state license fees to be levied on a per mile basis. This would provide a further incentive to limit automobile usage.

We could provide further tax incentives to employers to make it easy and appealing for workers to reduce their transportation load on the earth. In addition to providing tax credits for employer-sponsored carpool programs, we could offer tax credits to companies that provide showers and lockers for their employees. This would make commuting by foot or bicycle more comfortable and attractive. Moreover, if employees regularly engage in exercise, it is likely that companies would see a reduction in health insurance costs.

CAR SHARING PROGRAMS

Car sharing is another option. In car sharing programs, members reserve vehicles for a certain day and pay a fixed cost based on time and mileage. You often have a choice of vehicles, allowing you to rent a van for moving a piece of furniture and a hybrid car for a long drive. Reservations are usually made by phone or through the Internet.

Europe is the leader in car sharing where at least 70,000 people in 300 towns and cities in eight countries participate.[6] Dozens of cities in North America are planning or have implemented car sharing programs.[7]

There are many trails up the mountain, but in time they all reach the top.

Anya Seton

Condominium and cooperative housing developments offer excellent potential for car sharing programs. In such developments, there is already a home owners association in place that could manage a car sharing program. Since the housing units are close together, it would be very convenient for individual owners to use the vehicles. Likewise, car sharing programs would work well in livable towns and cities where homes are clustered together.

BICYCLE-FRIENDLY COMMUNITIES

In North America, we are overlooking a simple, effective form of transportation—the bicycle. We need to remap the infrastructure of our towns and cities to provide bicycle lanes and parking areas for bicycles. Clearly, it is less expensive to build bicycle lanes than cars, buses, and trains, together with the roads and railway tracks to support them. We could divert some of the funds we allocate for building new roads in North America to build bicycle transportation infrastructure.

Bicycles do not pollute the air or fill the airwaves with obnoxious noises. I believe the combination of safe bicycle lanes and showers at work would lead thousands of people out of their cars and onto their bicycles. I saw this first hand in the Netherlands, where people of all ages bicycled, rain or shine, in all manner of clothing. I was particularly impressed with the senior set, some dressed exquisitely, who cruised the bicycle lanes with confidence. During one month I worked in the Netherlands, I regularly came home to hear my husband report sheepishly, "Well, I got smoked on the bike by another grandma today."

As a bicyclist in Holland, you have the right of way—how appropriate! The relatively flat terrain of the Netherlands no doubt contributes to the fact that 30 percent of the trips are by bicycle.[8] With a bicycle and a train pass, you can easily live in the Netherlands without a car.

SIMPLICITY IN TRAVEL

I am one of those who never knows the direction of my journey until I have almost arrived.

Anna Louise Strong

People travel for many reasons, including business, recreation, education, and to visit family and friends. Often, we approach travel with a deprivation mindset. We focus on not having enough time. Our response is to try to squeeze in as much as possible on our trips. In some instances, we assume that we will not return to a specific destination, creating a desire to see as much as we can in this once-in-a-lifetime experience. Ironically, in our quest to see more, too often we experience less.

Our minds and bodies can assimilate only so much stimulation, so much excitement. If we overload our travel schedule, we disrupt the peace of mind required to be truly present when we visit new places and people. We become superficial voyeurs of another place or culture as the days of travel turn into a blur. When we return home, we remember the highlights but little else.

There is another way to travel, to engage your full self—mind, heart, and body—in the new environment. To travel well, you must move slowly and savor deeply.

When my husband and I visit foreign lands, we like to travel for a month at a time, preferably just in one country. If we don't have the time or money to travel for a month, we wait until we do. We enjoy concentrating on one culture, one foreign language, at a time. By doing so, we develop a sense of place for our destination, which starts feeling more and more like home to us as the weeks pass. In addition to visiting tourist sites, we spend a great deal of time living just as we would at home—shopping for food, cooking, taking walks, reading books, writing, visiting with friends. We often rent apartments rather than stay in hotels for this purpose. We become temporary residents of another country.

While month-long, single-country sojourns are our preference, it may not be your style. Indeed, you may need to try different types of trips to determine what works best for you. But I would strongly suggest that you think twice about visiting six countries in three weeks—or anything close to this schedule—even if those countries are right next to each other. Such travel is like watching a movie with the sound turned off. You only get a hint of what's going on.

For many people, foreign travel can be transformational, changing how we think of our lives and our world. When we spend time in different cultures, everything is new and fascinating. We start living in the present, because the present is so intriguing. We feel revitalized. Because you let go of what is familiar and routine for you, your inner mind is inclined to take a fresh look at your life—how you feel about what's going on and what direction you want to go next. As Joan Halifax explains in *The Fruitful Darkness*, "Whether we know it or not, we need to renew ourselves in territories that are fresh and wild. We need to come home through the body of alien lands." This may all take place without any conscious intention on your part. You may discover it only when you return home with renewed clarity about who you are and what is most important to you.

It is good to have an end to journey towards; but it is the journey that matters in the end.

Ursula K. Le Guin

I have experienced this first-hand through trips lasting a month or more to a variety of destinations, including Senegal (West Africa), the Galapagos Islands, the South Pacific islands of Fiji, Tahiti, and the Samoas, New Zealand, Bali, Italy, Ireland, and England. Each of these trips brought unexpected gifts of insight and peace of mind. My sense is that these experiences create in me a *deep knowing*, not only about myself but also about how connected we are with all other peoples.

Americans are sometimes criticized for being too insular—believing that we hold the most economic and political power, and therefore the rest of the world should take careful notes and follow in our footsteps. Rarely do we seek to learn from other cultures. This is not only arrogant, but incredibly shortsighted. It deprives us of the broader perspective of life that living in other countries can provide.

We have much to learn from other cultures. This was clearly evident to me when I conducted my simplicity study. Many

North American participants, when asked what led them to simplify their lives, mentioned that living in a foreign country influenced them to want to live more simply. In general, they experienced cultures that place far less value on materialism and enjoy richer family relationships, more community interaction, rewarding simple pleasures, and greater overall satisfaction in life.

It is for this reason—the power of travel for personal transformation—that I recommend that people take two to four months off every few years to live in a very different place, preferably a foreign country. Of course, if the experience of foreign cultures doesn't appeal to you, there is no reason to do it. But if it does, it can be highly rewarding on levels you may never have dreamed.

What man can imagine he may one day achieve.

Nancy Hale

Such a trip may appear impossible to you, but it is not. If you plan this adventure a year or more in advance, it's quite feasible. The two most commonly voiced objections to this idea are getting time off work and having enough money. Let's consider each of these objections.

If you work for others, you will need to approach your employer with a proposal to take a short leave of absence. Perhaps you can combine some vacation time with an unpaid leave. If you cooperate with your boss to make sure his or her needs are met while you are gone, and if you are a valued employee, it is highly likely that your employer will approve of your leave, especially if you submit your proposal a year or more in advance.

If you work for yourself, you *can* take a break from work if you plan ahead. You can let your clients know you are taking a short sabbatical. You can arrange for others to handle certain tasks while you are away. Believe it or not, the world will continue to run without you for those few months. You may miss out on some income during your time away, but you are unlikely to lose your business.

This travel adventure does not need to be a financial burden. If you have limited funds, consider renting out your home and finding a job while living abroad, or volunteer for an organization that covers your living expenses. If you plan ahead, you can also save money each month toward your trip. You could accept a short-term caretaker position in another country. Such arrangements are more available than you might think (see the Recommended Resources at the end of this lesson).

If your budget is very low, consider traveling to an inexpensive, developing country. This option may also offer a deeper experience because the culture of a developing country provides the most contrast to your own. This is, in fact, a trend in international travel. One in five tourists travels from an industrial country to a developing one, up from one in 13 in the mid-1970's.[9]

All this is possible if you plan ahead.

Traveling is seeing; it is the implicit that we travel by.

Cynthia Ozick

ECOTOURISM

For the first time, the number of international travelers exceeded 700 million in 2002, representing a 3.1 percent increase over travel in 2001, a surprising trend considering the September 11, 2001 terrorist acts.[10] As travelers and tourists, we have a responsibility to understand the social and environmental impacts of our travel. This concern has led to the development of a relatively new field called ecotourism. The International Ecotourism Society defines ecotourism as responsible travel that conserves the environment and sustains the well-being of local people. Preserving the local culture of the host country is also considered to be an objective of ecotourism.

There are many travel agencies and companies that attempt to fulfill ecotourism ideals. Some certification programs exist to identify which travel providers meet ecotourism criteria. However, the certification programs are inconsistent, with varying standards for qualifications. Some programs require only that a business pay a fee to obtain its "green" label.[11]

Fortunately, we don't need to rely on certification programs to travel responsibly. Much of it is common sense. To the extent that we stay in local accommodations, eat at local restaurants, and use local transport, we support local economies. Patronizing large, resource-intensive resorts owned by foreign investors is not an ideal way to contribute to the environmental health and well-being of the local people.

Since environmental preservation is essential to maintain tourism—people won't visit if the natural beauty is lost—it is in everyone's interests (locals and visitors alike) to maintain the environmental integrity of the host country. However, in some instances, local entrepreneurs develop travel programs that offer short term monetary gains but have long term environmental consequences.

Often it is up to the traveler to determine if a particular program or facility meets the standards of ecotourism. You can use the Internet to research these issues (see the Recommended Resources at the end of this lesson). In addition to information provided by destination web sites and umbrella travel organizations, you can contact a travel provider directly by email with specific questions.

Waste is a spiritual thing and harms the soul as well as the pocketbook.

Kathleen Norris

One way to contribute to the well-being of local people is to participate in community-based travel programs, in which travelers work together with the locals on sustainable projects designed to improve the economic health or quality of life of the local population. There is a vast array of opportunities of this nature, ranging from extensive volunteer work to less involved exchanges with locals as part of a broader travel program (see the Recommended Resources at the end of this lesson).

CONCLUSION

Transporting ourselves from one place to another does not have to be an expensive, bothersome experience. We need to take a fresh look at this critical aspect of lives to see how we can enhance our pleasure while reducing our impact on the earth. We also need to work with different levels of government to obtain the infrastructure we need to make alternatives to the automobile a reality.

Visiting foreign cultures can be a richly rewarding experience and source of personal transformation. If you are drawn to such travel, do not let perceived limitations stand in your way. Just do it.

LESSON ASSIGNMENTS

FROM YOUR PERSONAL VIEWPOINT . . .

1. What does your transportation profile look like? Make a list of the different forms of transportation you use (for example, driving an automobile, walking, riding on a bus, bicycling) in a typical week. List the approximate amount of time and mileage spent in each form of transportation. See the Transportation Inventory on page 203. The purpose of this exercise is to be consciously aware of your transportation choices.
2. Describe the degree of stress or pleasure associated with each form of transportation you use.
3. Calculate the number of gallons of gasoline you use each year by multiplying the number of miles driven by the miles per gallon your automobile gets. For example, if you drive 10,000 miles a year and get 20 miles to the gallon, you have consumed 500 gallons of gasoline. However, if some of those miles were shared with another person in the car (for example, by car pooling to work or taking a family vacation trip by car), you should include only your prorata share. So, for example, if 5,000 of your 10,000 miles were shared with one other person, your share of that is 2,500 miles, not the full 5,000. In this example, your net gallons of gasoline for the year would be 375 rather than 500. Do not be concerned if you don't know the exact number of miles you drive alone versus with others. Use your best guess estimates. This calculation will give you your base level. If you find ways to reduce the total miles you drive, you can chart your progress accordingly.
4. If you would like to make some changes in your transportation uses, what would those be? How might you best accomplish your objectives? Are your desired transportation choices dependent on a change in your work or home location? Refer to the Time Inventory you completed in Lesson 5 to determine how any transportation changes might fit into your overall schedule.
5. Have you traveled to foreign countries? If so, what are your most memorable or pleasurable experiences from

Responsibility is the price every man must pay for freedom.

Edith Hamilton

5600 mi
35 mpg
160 gal

those trips? What value did you receive from those trips? If you travel to other countries in the future, would you like to do it any differently? If so, what changes would you make?

LOOKING AT THE BIGGER PICTURE . . .

6. What is being done in your community to offer alternatives to automobile transportation? What specific steps could your community take to expand transportation options for everyone?
7. What type of tax incentives do you think would be appropriate to encourage more sustainable transportation alternatives? What would you personally be willing to do or pay to make these alternatives a reality?

Only in growth, reform, and change, paradoxically enough, is true security to be found.

Anne Morrow Lindbergh

LIFEWORK ASSIGNMENTS

1. Experiment with different transportation options. For example, you might try getting by without a car for a one-week period. This may not be a permanent option, but it is useful to see how you react to other methods of moving about. For example, you might be surprised to find that you enjoy the relaxation of taking the bus instead of driving in congested traffic, or that walking to do an errand is pleasurable in and of itself.
2. If you decide to incorporate new transportation options, come up with a detailed plan of incremental steps to accomplish your goals. For example, if you want to try carpooling to work, start by arranging for a carpool once a week. See how that goes and then add other days as you and your car buddies adjust to the new routine.

ANNUAL CHECK-UP

1. Review the Transportation Inventory you completed the prior year. Have you made any significant changes? If so, what are the positive and negative impacts of those changes?
2. What are your transportation goals for the coming year?

Come up with a plan to implement any changes you desire to make.

RECOMMENDED RESOURCES

BOOKS

Asphalt Nation: How the Automobile Took over America, and How We Can Take It Back by Jane Holtz Kay (Berkeley: University of California Press, Reprint 1998). Examines the growth of automobile use in America and its impact on our culture, the environment, and the economy. Kay also suggests economic, political, architectural, and personal solutions to "car glut."

Volunteer Vacations: Short-Term Adventures That Will Benefit You and Others by Bill McMillon, Doug Cutchins, and Anne Geissinger (Chicago: Chicago Review Press, 8th edition, 2003). Resource guide for volunteer vacations that offer culturally enriching, service-oriented travel experiences. Includes profiles of over 200 organizations.

MISCELLANEOUS

Car Sharing Network [www.carsharing.net] offers an excellent introduction to car sharing. It includes a database of existing car sharing programs, online discussion groups, media articles, and other resources.

Crooked Trails [www.crookedtrails.com] is a community-based, nonprofit travel organization that sponsors eco-tours to developing countries. Visits to other countries include participation in the daily life of indigenous peoples—their work and culture. The programs are designed to facilitate cultural exchanges that allow visitors and hosts to share in each other's lives.

The International Ecotourism Society [www.ecotourism.org] was founded in 1990 to foster a synergy between outdoor travel entrepreneurs, researchers, and conservationists. Its goal is to assist professionals who want to make ecotourism a genuine tool for conservation and sustainable development. It offers many resources, including a speaker's bureau, research library, and a membership network.

Servas [www.servas.org] is an international, nonprofit peace organization in which travelers and hosts share their daily lives with people from other cultures. The focus of the program is cultural exchange and mutual learning.

World Tourism Organization [www.world-tourism.org], an intergovernmental organization vested by the United Nations, serves as a global forum for tourism policy issues and a practical source of tourism know-how and statistics. Its central and decisive role is to promote the development of responsible, sustainable, and universally accessible tourism.

NOTE: *Additions and updates to these resources can be found on The Simplicity Resource Guide at www.gallagherpress.com/pierce.*

LESSON 8

AWAKENING THE SPIRIT WITHIN YOU

SPIRITUALITY AND SIMPLICITY

In *The Pierce Simplicity Study*, I asked people to describe their spiritual beliefs and experiences and any links between these beliefs and their attraction to simplicity. Most respondents spoke enthusiastically of the value of an inner life and the interplay between simplicity and spirituality. Seventy percent of them rated spirituality (or some expression of an inner life) as a high priority.

The terms *spirituality* and the *inner life* cover a wide range of experiences—from organized religious practices to less formally structured spiritual awareness and experiences (such as yoga, meditation, journal writing, and spiritually-related reading), artistic creativity, self-reflection, and intuitive knowledge. Additionally, some people view their experiences in nature as both the source and expression of their spirituality. Others have no interest in anything spiritual or religious, but resonate with concepts of personal fulfillment, introspection, and inner growth.

There are certain common threads in the belief systems of those who find spiritual development and religion personally meaningful. One involves belief in a higher being—either God, or a god or gods, or the presence of a force greater than ourselves. Some believe that we are somehow connected with the earth and each other in a manner that is beyond the realm of our five senses. It is this feeling of connection that propels us to look outside ourselves and develop true compassion and love for other people and the earth.

In considering the dynamic interplay between simplicity and spirituality, it is not always clear which comes first. Living simply engenders a greater appreciation for the inner world and vice versa. For some people, the two concepts are so intertwined that it is difficult to distinguish one from the other. Here are some representative statements from the participants in my simplicity study:

> Living this way [simply] has brought me closer to realizing that each moment is a spiritual, divine moment. I can't separate it out from anything else I do.

> I think that my previously simple lifestyle was good preparation for active spiritual practice, and may have had something to do with putting me in a receptive frame of mind.

> I see these inner-growth/spiritual reachings as the cause, not the consequence, of my turning to a simpler lifestyle.

> I'm not real sure what happened first, but I think there was a spiritual surrender that opened the door to simplification. There followed three years of emptying out on all levels and another three years of "filling up," mostly spiritually. Life has become a joyful adventure—a conscious adventure.

The externals are simply so many props; everything we need is within us.

Etty Hillesum

There is a rational basis for the complementary relationship between simplicity and spirituality. When you rid your life of unneeded possessions, unwanted social commitments, and excessive work-related stress, you create a quiet space within yourself for reflection. Inner reflection awakens in us a sense of soul or spirit. In truth, we are all born spiritual beings, but then we subsequently bury our spirituality under a mountain of work, materialism, busyness, and stress.

When we live simply, we live more lightly, with fewer distractions that interfere with our true nature, which is, in part, spiritual. Our relationship to material things changes. Rather than being consumed by materialism, we surround ourselves with only those possessions we truly need or genuinely cherish. Inevitably, this is less than what North American culture would have us believe is necessary for the *good life*. When we reduce the hold that materialism has on our lives, a door opens to other dimensions—relationships, artistic and intellectual endeavors, and spirituality, to name a few. Just as eliminating excessive materialism can lead to enhanced spirituality, a heightened spiritual awareness induces us to keep our material lives in balance.

There are certain spiritual beliefs that lead us to live more simply. If we believe we are intimately connected with all other life forms in the universe, then love, compassion, and respect will follow naturally (unless we are masochists). We will be motivated to live more simply so that others may simply live, because the *others* are a part of us. Boundaries between us dissolve.

I want to take only what I need, not because my taking less will necessarily provide greater resources to the truly poor, but out of honor and respect for people who truly do not have enough.

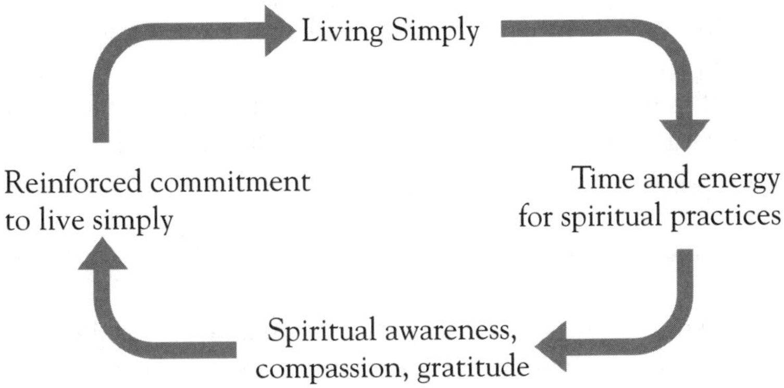

Prayer is an exercise of the spirit, as thought is of the mind.

Mary F. Smith

UNEARTHING YOUR SPIRITUALITY

You do not create your spirituality. In truth, you can only discover it since it is already there, inside of you. Your awareness of your spiritual nature can be a vital, enriching component of the human experience, but it's up to you to make it a part of your conscious life and decide what form it shall take. There are many ways to accomplish this. One method is the simple practice of silence and solitude.

Ideally, you would set aside 30 minutes each day to be alone and quiet. You may want to spend that time writing in a journal, meditating, taking a walk in nature, or just sitting still. Reading the morning newspaper or engaging in similar forms of external stimulation should be reserved for another time. It doesn't matter what you think about, or if you think of anything at all. The only requirements are silence and solitude. There are many guides and books on meditation, journal writing, and walking in nature. But you can start with something as simple as sitting on your back porch listening to the birds sing. Eventually, you will be inspired to go deeper, but don't rush it. Let your spirituality surface slowly, at your own pace.

I can already hear you say, "Where on earth am I going to find an extra 30 minutes in my day? You obviously haven't spent any time in this household!" True, there are no extra minutes in any of our days. Thus, your task is to replace 30 minutes of your current routine with 30 minutes of silence and solitude. If you are, like most North Americans, sleep deprived, don't steal further from this important need. One approach is to go to sleep 30 minutes earlier than normal—watch one less television show or read one less magazine. Then, get up that much earlier, when other family members may still be slumbering. You will be fresh from your dream state, and the details of the upcoming day have not yet cluttered your mind. This is an ideal time to create your oasis of silence and solitude. But it's not the only time, and if another time of day works better for you, by all means, do it then.

It is in our idleness, in our dreams, that the submerged truth sometimes comes to the top.

Virginia Woolf

The most important thing about this practice is consistency. It may take you as long as a month before you perceive any benefits of daily silence and solitude. You will begin to experience more clarity in your life with less effort. Your internal rhythms will slow, giving you a sense of inner peace. The impact will be on your life as a whole. Your actual practice of silence and solitude may feel rather mundane or even boring, but that doesn't mean it isn't working its wonders.

Of course, there is nothing about simplicity that dictates or prescribes any particular forms of spiritual practice. Simplicity just makes it easier to embrace what works for you.

Spiritual practices are as diverse and distinct as individual people. In addition to practices associated with organized religions—praying in community or alone, listening to a preacher, minister, priest, or rabbi, Buddhist meditation, Quaker silent prayer meetings—there are unlimited forms of informal, communal, and solitary spiritual practices. Reading and reflecting on a spiritually-inspired book, gasping in awe at a beautiful sight in nature, and gardening can all be spiritual practices.

COMPASSION AND GRATITUDE

I have observed certain spiritual characteristics in people who live simply: compassion and gratitude. Compassion is evident in the deep caring that people who live simply have for other people and for this planet we call home. This compassion for the earth leads many people who practice simplicity to be conscious of the earth's limited resources and committed to sustainability practices.

When we live simply, we slow down the pace of our lives, which, in turn, frees up time and energy to give to other people. Living simply also calms our minds, expanding our mental and emotional capacities to focus on the welfare of others. Obviously, if we are mentally exhausted, emotionally drained, and just generally stressed out, we have little left to give to others.

Gratitude is a major theme in the lives of people who live simply. On a material level, this naturally evolves when we reduce our material load to things we truly need or cherish. With fewer things in our personal environment, we notice and appreciate what we do have to a greater degree. Simplicity and spiritual practices beget inner joy, which, in turn, leads us to be grateful for everything in our lives—our loved ones, a delicious meal, and other simple pleasures in life.

Gratitude weighs heavily on us only when we no longer feel it.

Contesse Diane

One of my favorite books is *How to Want What You Have* by psychologist Timothy Miller. In this book, Miller describes in detail how the practices of compassion, attention, and gratitude lead to deep happiness and immense joy. In my view, this book does a brilliant job of capturing the spiritual aspects of simplicity. I recommend it highly.

NATURE AS A SPIRITUAL PRACTICE

When our local simplicity study group met to discuss spirituality, much of the conversation focused on experiences in nature. Many feel that being in the presence of nature's majesty invokes a sense of the divine—a glimpse of higher and deeper levels of being.

There is a long history of connection between spirituality and the earth. For example, the cycles and gifts of nature are essential to Native American spirituality. In the spiritual practices of many of the earliest peoples, the Earth was revered as Mother—literally recognizing that it is the earth's bounty that nurtures and supports us, the sun, the moon, rain, even thunder and wind. We're just one part of the vast mystery in which we all take part. Over the centuries, philosophers, artists, and writers—William Wordsworth, Henry David Thoreau, and others—have found spiritual solace in nature, revivifying instincts that early peoples acknowledged in daily rituals of gratitude.

Most of us today have a sense of that mystery. I remember as a teenager on camping trips feeling moved by the exquisite beauty of California's High Sierra mountains. I had the overwhelming sense that God was near as I hiked along dirt trails shadowed by tall pine trees. I still feel a divine presence during solo walks in the woods or along the seashore in the early morning.

In *The Art of Travel*, Alain de Botton explores the depth of experience when in the presence of the *sublime*—a natural landscape that is powerful and noble while leaving no doubt of our relative smallness and vulnerability. It is an expansive feeling of pleasure, awe, and respect. It is but a small leap to associate such natural majesty with a compelling belief in God or a higher divine presence. In Alain de Botton's words, "The mountains and valleys spontaneously suggest that the planet was built by something other than our own hands, by a force greater than we could gather, long before we were born, and set to continue long after our extinction."

Nature's silence is its one remark, and every flake of world is a chip off that old mute and immutable block.

Annie Dillard

But one does not need to climb high mountain peaks to experience the spirit in nature. We live in and are surrounded by nature. All we need to do is open our eyes. One of the people featured in my book, *Choosing Simplicity*, describes such an experience:

> Longing for more of the natural world was one of the first things that stirred thoughts of voluntary simplicity in me. I was working in a 40-story office building in 1993 and it had been a stressful, hectic day. I was running to deliver a file to another office when I looked up. In front of me was a conference room with the door ajar and through that door I could see the most stunning, vibrant sunset through floor-to-ceiling windows. I literally stopped moving and stared through that doorway until, looking around to make sure no one saw where I was going, I went into the room and closed the door. The experience reminded me of the medieval monks who prayed in cells that were plain on three walls and painted with a beautiful, inspirational spiritual scene on the fourth wall. I felt like that conference room was temporarily transformed into a spiritual space that evening.

It is interesting to note that 30 percent of the simplicity study participants spend extensive time in nature while another 33 percent spend moderate time in nature. The gifts of simplicity—more unstructured time and energy—make this possible.

CREATIVITY AS A SPIRITUAL PRACTICE

In *The Artist's Way*, Julia Cameron opens her book with the statement, "Art is a spiritual transaction." She likens the practice of creating art to a pilgrimage, an act of faith. It compels the artist to travel to an undetermined destination, not knowing what she will find, bringing with her only the hope and faith that something lovely will result. The act of creating often feels like leaping off the top of a mountain. At best, it is a mysterious process in which a creation forms unexpectedly, never on schedule, and often at the weirdest times and places.

We must accept that this creative pulse within us is God's creative pulse itself.

Joseph Chilton Pearce

Walking is my creative muse. I often walk to town (30 minutes each way) during my mid-day writing break. I'll be walking along minding my own business (which at that moment is daydreaming, not writing) and without any forewarning, a brilliant idea (or so it seems in my endorphin-induced state) will appear on my mental radar screen. I didn't ask for it; in most instances, I had yet to formulate the question when the answer shows up. It is understandably tempting to associate this mysterious nature of creativity with the spiritual realm.

The way artists describe their creative processes is uncannily similar to the way spiritual leaders describe their experiences—the feelings of being transfixed or transported, proceeding through a dark night of the soul, or sensing a mystical force working through them. Creating art can truly be a transcendental experience.

Art, like spirituality, is expressed in many forms, from a painting of fine art to the visual display of colors and textures of food on a dinner plate. Of course, dance, drama, music, and writing are art forms. There are even moments in running a business that are as creative as the finest musical score. Creativity happens when we leap off the mountain into the unknown—when we reach deep within ourselves to discover that which we did not know—to create something uniquely beautiful.

In Hal Zina Bennett's book, *Write from the Heart*, he observes that "Few of us any longer think of creativity as a frivolous activity, or as something only self-indulgent, 'arty' people take seriously. We're recognizing that it nurtures us, at a time when humanity is very much in need of spiritual support. We're realizing that our creative efforts are a way to bring us all a little closer to ourselves and, in doing so, renew the spirit of humankind."

CONCLUSION

If we go down into ourselves we find that we posses exactly what we desire.

Simone Weil

Our inner selves journey over an infinite landscape—spirituality, nature, and creativity. These spiritual potentialities provide opportunities for transcendence, a deep sense of fulfillment, and immense joy. Clearly, not all time spent in nature, artistic endeavors, or even in church are spiritual experiences. But the potential is there.

To the extent we develop our inner worlds, our external lives will flow more freely. As I've said, simplicity, in its essence, is an inside job. It's not something you can pick up from reading a few books on how to simplify your life. It must come from within and from your own labors and commitment. It requires self-knowledge. Once we quiet the roaring clamor within, that self-knowledge will be clear as a bell. We will feel less confused about the complex choices that confront us. What type of work to do? Where to live? How to enhance our personal relationships? How to balance our work and personal lives?

The answers are all there for the taking. In the assignments that follow, you will have an opportunity to practice inner simplicity and benefit from its wondrous gifts.

LESSON ASSIGNMENTS

FROM YOUR PERSONAL VIEWPOINT . . .

1. Do you see yourself as a spiritual or religious person? What does that mean to you? Describe your spiritual or religious practices.
2. Do you spend any time in nature? If so, describe your ex-

periences. Do you see any connection between being in nature and your spirituality? If so, describe what you feel.

3. Do you engage in any creative activities or practices? If so, describe your experiences. What, if any, connection is there between your creative activities and your spirituality?
4. Do you have other experiences that speak of an inner life? Don't limit yourself to what is discussed in this lesson. Describe those experiences and what they mean to you.
5. Think about what in your life contributes to your sense of inner peace and what interferes with it. How can you modify your life patterns to enhance your sense of inner peace?
6. Do you sense any connection between spirituality and living simply? If so, describe what that connection means to you.

No journey carries one far unless, as it extends into the world around us, it goes an equal distance into the world within.

Lillian Smith

LOOKING AT THE BIGGER PICTURE . . .

7. Does your culture place a high value on an inner life? Describe ways it does or does not.
8. Think of social and public policies that would support the opportunities for people to experience inner simplicity. Describe them in as much detail as you can.
9. Do you feel that spirituality has a role in furthering global peace and justice? If so, describe how spirituality might impact these global issues.

LIFEWORK ASSIGNMENTS

1. Start a gratitude journal. Each day, write down three things for which you are grateful. Make them specific to that day. For example, instead of writing, "I am grateful to have a loving husband," you might write, "I am grateful for my loving husband who helped me fix my computer problem today."
2. Practice your silence and solitude exercises. Start with 5 or 10 minutes and build up gradually to 30 minutes each day. Morning works best for many people, but pick a time that works well for you. Meditate, write in your journal,

practice yoga, walk in nature, sit quietly, do whatever, so long as you are alone and quiet.

3. Take a solo nature hike in a safe area. A frequently travelled trail can be relatively safe. Also, if you sprain an ankle, you want to be sure that someone will be coming along shortly to help. Another approach is to go on a solo hike with a buddy—two of you can hike together, staying close in proximity, but each quiet in his own world.
4. If you are drawn to artistic creativity, set aside some time each week to practice your art. If you are new to the medium you choose, consider taking a class to get you started. As you progress in your learning, ask yourself if, and how, your art connects to your spiritual self.
5. If you have an interest in growing things, consider reading some of the many books on the spiritual aspects of gardening. Your library should have some. Think about your own gardening experiences. Is there a connection there to your spirituality?

Religion is a bridge to the spiritual, but the spiritual lies beyond religion.

Rachel Naomi Remen

ANNUAL CHECK-UP

1. Review your spiritual practices during the last year. What have you found to be most rewarding? What would you like to continue with, add, or remove from your life?
2. Review the lifework assignments to see if anything interests you, or come up with your own spiritual adventure.

RECOMMENDED RESOURCES

BOOKS

The Artist's Way: A Spiritual Path to Higher Creativity by Julia Cameron (New York: J.P. Tarcher, 10th edition, 2002). Bestselling book guides the reader through 12 weeks of reflections and exercises designed to open up the paths to creativity. You don't need to be an artist to benefit from this book. Cameron recommends a daily practice of *morning pages*, a free-from writing exercise, which can also serve as a spiritual practice.

Care of the Soul: A Guide for Cultivating Depth and Sacredness in Everyday Life by Thomas Moore (New York: Harper Perennial,

Reprinted 1994). Former Catholic monk and therapist writes about the loss of soul in modern society and suggests ways to nurture the soul, cultivate depth, and develop inner peace in today's world.

Epicurean Simplicity by Stephanie Mills (Washington, D.C.: Island Press/Shearwater Books, 2002). Memoir/essay about author's experience living simply on 35 acres in the Upper Midwest. The author, a writer and speaker on the issues of ecology and social change, describes simple pleasures, especially delight in the natural world, and shares her reflections on deep ecology and voluntary simplicity.

Freedom of Simplicity by Richard J. Foster (New York: Harper, 1998). Christian-oriented book proposing a biblical basis for the principles of voluntary simplicity. Offers guidance on how to live simply in a complex world using the power of prayer and solitude.

How to Want What You Have: Discovering the Magic and Grandeur of Ordinary Existence by Timothy Miller, Ph.D. (New York: Avon, 1996). Clinical psychologist explores the human tendency to always want more and the lack of connection between material wealth and happiness. Offers an alternative path to happiness, based on the practices of compassion, attention, and gratitude.

Inner Simplicity: 100 Ways to Regain Peace and Nourish Your Soul by Elaine St. James (New York: Hyperion, 1995). Short essays of a how-to nature focusing on the inner life of simplicity.

Lilabean: A Story of Simplicity for Grown-up Girls by K.C. White (Elizabeth City, NC: Bean Pot Press, 2002). A delightful storybook written in verse detailing one woman's evolution from being overwhelmed with clutter and not enough time to creating a life of simplicity and joy. This book would be a great gift for a woman friend who is simplifying her life.

Ordinary People as Monks and Mystics: Lifestyles for Self-Discovery by Marsha Sinetar (New York: Paulist Press, 1986). Presents real life stories of people who have explored their inner selves as part of the process of becoming whole. While the book does not focus specifically on voluntary simplicity, most of the people featured live simply.

Plain Living: A Quaker Path to Simplicity by Catherine Whitmire (Notre Dame, IN: Sorin Books, 2001). Using the wisdom of present-day Quakers and Quaker elders, Whitmire explores the dimensions of living a simple and spiritually enriching lifestyle, including ways to create a world free of physical and spiritual clutter.

Simple Abundance: A Daybook of Comfort and Joy by Sarah Ban Breathnach (New York: Warner, 1995). Bestselling book of short essays written for women. Explores themes such as harmony, gratitude, authentic creative expression, and spirituality.

Simplicity: Finding Peace by Uncluttering Your Life by Kim Thomas (Nashville, TN: Broadman & Holman, 1999). Discusses simplicity from a religious point of view, as a tool to enhance one's relationship to God. Reviews the benefits of simplicity as it applies to the physical world, the relational and emotional world, and the spiritual world.

To Have or To Be? by Erich Fromm (New York: Continuum, Reissued 1996). Author of *The Art of Loving* explores the differences between the *having* mode, based on our relationship to things, and the *being* mode, based on our relationship to other people, the earth, and ourselves.

Wherever You Go There You Are: Mindfulness Meditation in Everyday Life by Jon Kabat-Zinn (New York: Hyperion, 1994). Explores practice of meditation in depth. Offers guidelines for cultivating practice of mindfulness.

Write from the Heart: Unleashing the Power of Your Creativity by Hal Zina Bennett (Novato, CA: New World Library, 2nd edition, 2001). Explores the relationship between spirituality and creativity for writers. New edition includes helpful exercises to expand your creative powers.

NOTE: *Additions and updates to these resources can be found on The Simplicity Resource Guide at www.gallagherpress.com/pierce.*

LESSON 9

MINDING YOUR HEALTH AND WELL-BEING

HEALTH AND SIMPLICITY

At its best, simplicity embodies the basics, the essentials of the good life. Your health and well-being are as basic as it gets. It is through our bodies that we feel most connected with the earth. We eat food grown in the earth's soil. We breathe in fresh air. Our senses witness the earth's beauty—we *see* the spectacular colors and textures in plants and trees, we *hear* a bird's beautiful song, we *feel* the smooth caress of water when we bathe.

When you live simply, you have time and energy to engage in healthful practices—taking in nutritious foods, appropriate exercise, sufficient sleep, and hopefully unpolluted air. You also develop the mindfulness necessary to determine what your body needs.

Living in harmony with our natural rhythms is a marvelous fringe benefit of living simply. Once a reporter asked me, "What has made the biggest impact in your life as a result of simplifying?" Without giving much thought to the question, I immediately responded, "Sleep." I now get enough sleep, in sharp contrast to my years as a lawyer, dragging myself out of bed each morning after being awake half the night fretting over some work issue. Now I go to sleep when I'm tired and I wake up when my mind and body are ready to embrace the day, typically eight to nine hours later. I do not use an alarm clock unless I have an early morning appointment, which is rare. To me, waking up after a good night's sleep is one of life's finest pleasures.

FOOD AND DRINK

It is not unusual for people who simplify their lives to experience changes in their eating and drinking habits. For example, many participants in my simplicity study reported a decrease in their use of caffeine and alcohol. They explained that it happened naturally, without force or discipline. This makes sense. When you live simply, you engage in mindful living, paying attention, focusing on what is happening in the present. So, for example, if you feel terrible the morning after drinking too much alcohol—and you have the presence of mind to acknowledge it to yourself—it may only be a matter of time before you reduce or eliminate alcohol from your diet. After all, psychologists concur that we have a natural, inborn desire to seek pleasure and avoid pain.

This does not mean that drinking coffee or alcohol is contrary to simplicity. While either in excess can be damaging, we also associate positive experiences with them. The caffeine in coffee can jump start your brain, giving you a boost of energy. Alcohol can induce a state of relaxation and a sense of well-being. Some medical researchers claim that drinking frequent, moderate amounts of alcohol lowers your risk of heart disease.[1]

The body is wiser than its inhabitants.

Erica Jong

It's important to be mindful of your body's reactions to substances you take in and to refrain from ingesting substances that result in negative reactions, whether coffee, alcohol, sugar, wheat, dairy food, or any other substance. Sometimes it is a matter of degree. For example, my body gets along very well on one cup of coffee a day, but two or three cups gives me the jitters, followed by fatigue and sometimes depression. Since I find it difficult to limit myself to one cup only, I try to avoid it altogether.

When people have the presence of mind to really listen to their bodies, they seem to naturally cut back on meat and heavily processed foods, favoring natural, nutrient-rich fresh foods, vegetables, and fruits. I suspect this is because our bodies feel better when we eat healthy foods.

It is interesting that 32 percent of the participants in my simplicity study eat a vegetarian or vegan diet, while another 51 percent include some meat but otherwise focus on fresh, unprocessed foods. Many vegetarians are motivated not only by health issues, but also by their concern for preserving the earth's resources and their compassion for animals raised in American factory farms. In *Diet for a New America* and *The Food Revolution*, John Robbins presents a compelling three-pronged rationale—based on health, the environment, and animal rights—to support a vegetarian diet. While I find his arguments persuasive, I don't believe a vegetarian diet is indispensable to a life lived simply. The essence of living simply is living authentically from within rather than adhering to a set of rules imposed from the outside. If you feel drawn to a vegetarian diet because of health concerns, compassion for animals, or concern for the earth, then it's a good choice for you. But it *is* a choice; the simplicity police will not be banging on your door if you eat meat.

Deciding what to eat is complicated by the vast array of conflicting advice by experts. We are told by some to eat a high protein diet, while others recommend a high carbohydrate, low-fat diet. Sugar and fat compete for being the most harmful foods. At least there is a consensus that more nutrients are retained in less processed food.

We also know that American diets are dangerously unhealthy. Lack of exercise alone cannot account for the fact that nearly two out of three North Americans are overweight or excessively fat, or that obesity has increased by 50 percent during the last decade.[2] Whether we eat the wrong foods or simply too much volume of food is a matter of debate. In the end, we must each do our own research and experimentation with food choices.

As I see it, every day you do one of two things: build health or produce disease in yourself.

Adelle Davis

Preparing and cooking food generally plays a significant role in the lives of people who live simply. Learning to be mindful while preparing food offers a sensual pleasure of its own—focusing on the colors and textures of food. Cooking from raw ingredients is one of the most nurturing things you can do for yourself and your loved ones. Preparing meals uses all of you—your body, your mind, and your heart.

For those inclined to grow a vegetable garden, the rewards are substantial. Many who grow their own food and prepare it mindfully report that it reconnects them with what's essential and basic in life. For them it becomes the very essence of simple living. Delicious food and an intimate awareness of the earth's abundant nature can add much joy to life.

Mindful cooking leads to mindful, relaxed eating. If food preparation is a relaxing, sensual experience, you are unlikely to follow it with a rushed, distracted meal. However, if you watch TV or read during your meals, you and your stomach will hardly notice what you are eating. You are missing out on one of life's finest, simplest pleasures—enjoying the taste of food while you are actually eating it!

EXERCISE

I noticed some interesting exercise patterns among the participants of my simplicity study. There was a striking lack of highly competitive sports, such as tennis and golf, and a high rate of non-competitive athletic activity such as walking, bicycling, hiking, or kayaking. It appears that when we slow down the pace of our lives, we naturally gravitate to more relaxing, calming physical activities. Perhaps we lose the desire for the adrenaline rush produced by athletic competition.

Where there is laughter there is always more health than sickness.

Phyllis Bottome

Another interesting finding is that many of the study participants engage in exercise primarily to serve a purpose other than maintaining good health. For example, people walk or bicycle to work as a form of transportation, or they hike for the sensual pleasure of experiencing nature directly. They focus their attention on what they are doing rather than distract themselves with reading or watching TV while working out on a treadmill. Exercise is a natural, pleasurable part of their lives, not a boring chore to fit into an already overscheduled daily routine. Like our diets, it is important to be aware of the effects of exercise on our bodies in order to understand how much and what types of exercise best suit us.

In Lesson 5, I discuss how the act of walking gives us the perception that time is expanding. Walking and bicycling are forms of exercise we can easily incorporate into our daily lives, unless we live in isolated suburban or rural communities. We can walk or bicycle to do errands, possibly to transport ourselves to work, or to visit friends. By combining our transportation and exercise needs, we live a more integrated life in which our actions serve multiple priorities—like combining work and play, nature and spirituality, or transportation and exercise. In addition to the benefits of exercise and transportation, walking and bicycling conserve money and environmental resources.

MENTAL AND EMOTIONAL HEALTH

Mental and emotional health is an essential component of well-being. Meditation, yoga, and similar practices are not only spiritually nourishing, they also contribute to your mental and emotional health. It is well established, of course, that regular physical exercise also helps us maintain our mental and emotional health.[3]

Moreover, the entire infrastructure of our lives—our work, our relationships, how we spend our days—has an enormous impact on our mental and emotional health. Depression and anxiety in North America may be more the result of living frenetically and seeking happiness through materialism than of any intrinsic psychological shortcomings. A simple lifestyle allows us to take a closer look at how we spend our time, what benefits we derive from our activities, and how we can design our daily lives to maximize health and wellness.

We all of us deserve happiness or none of us does.

Mary Gordon

HEALTH FOR EVERYONE

One of the things that becomes increasingly clear as we simplify our lives is how interdependent our planet is, of how our personal lifestyles affect others, even on the other side of the world. Collectively, our health and well-being are dependent on planet Earth's health, for if we are each to enjoy pure water, good air, and nutritious foods, we must make certain that we are not doing things to impede our planet's capacity for providing these. As our simpler life develops, we slow down and become increasingly aware of the subtler implications of this interdependence.

It is not always easy to figure out how I, just one person, can honor the interdependence we on this planet share. In this lesson we'll explore the dynamics of these interdependencies as they relate to health and well-being.

First, some facts. Today, over one billion people, or one-sixth of the world's population, are chronically undernourished.[4] Twenty thousand people die each day from hunger or hunger related causes, three-fourths of them children under the age of five.[5] The good news is that this figure is down from 41,000 deaths per day 25 years ago. The bad news is that 20,000 is still a lot of people, almost seven times the number of people who died in the terrorist attacks on September 11, 2001. It totals 7.3 million deaths per year. If we were to let the full weight of that number sink into our hearts and consciousness, it would be difficult to continue living life as we know it. If we knew the people who are starving to death like we know our friends and neighbors, we simply would not let it happen.

Adequate food production and distribution involves complex economic and political issues and is increasingly threatened by various environmental factors, such as soil erosion, aquifer depletion, and climate change. Even so, the world actually produces enough food for everyone, in excess of 2,700 calories per day per person on the planet.[6] However, we feed almost half the world's grain to livestock, which in turn produce a relatively small amount of food value compared to the grain fed to them. There are countless other factors, including rapid population growth, that contribute to world hunger. Similarly, insufficient water, both for drinking and sanitation, threatens the lives of millions of people. Numerous private and public organizations, including several United Nations organizations, are working to solve these complex problems, but it will take years to completely eradicate global hunger.

The first freedom of man, I contend, is the freedom to eat.

Eleanor Roosevelt

So, what can we do? We can do many things. First, we can educate ourselves about how our lifestyles—the way we live in North America—affects the earth overall and, consequently, the health conditions of people in developing countries. For example, per capita resource utilization and waste generation in North America is over 10 times that of developing countries. If all people lived as we do, we would need at least three planets the size of earth to sustain us.[7] By taking more than our fair share of resources, we put others at risk for their very lives. This is discussed in more depth in Lesson 12.

As mentioned above, John Robbins' books, *Diet for a New America* and *The Food Revolution*, provide specific information on how our meat-based diets deplete natural resources—such as water and croplands for grain—that are (or ultimately will be) needed to feed others. If we eliminate or reduce the meat in our diets, we honor this interdependence.

As discussed in Lesson 8, compassion and gratitude seem to expand with simplicity. As we become more conscious of what great abundance we in North America have, we may feel a desire to share our abundance with those who have less. You can do this in any number of ways, from volunteering your time to giving money to an organization that provides food and health services to those who cannot afford it.

Most of us are not wealthy, and it can be difficult to donate money when we have trouble enough paying the bills. But wealth is a relative concept. Over one billion people in the world live on $1 a day or less.[8] On a global scale, North Americans are very wealthy.

I have a vision: What if every family in North America contributed a monthly amount equal to their cable or satellite television bill to an organization whose mission is to help people obtain adequate food and water? If we can afford cable TV, we can't be too poor. It also represents a luxury when considering basic human needs. A wide range of humanitarian organizations exist, from local soup kitchens to organizations that work to further self-reliance in developing countries.

The test of a civilization is in the way that it cares for its members.

Pearl S. Buck

We may be disinclined to do this, believing that the solutions require larger, systemic political and economic changes. But while we wait for global politics to solve the problem, 20,000 people die every day. We can choose not to contribute because we fear the money may not be used wisely or that foreign governmental corruption will prevent the funds from getting to the people who need it, or we can keep searching until we find an organization whose work we believe in. If this idea appeals to you, it's easy to implement. It just takes some research to decide which organization to work with (see the Recommended Resources at the end of this lesson for information on charitable organizations). Why not challenge your friends and family to do the same?

But, again, don't feel you *should* or *have* to give in this way. If you don't feel motivated to do so, don't sweat it. Simplicity is not about imposing rules on anyone. Perhaps you will feel motivated sometime in the future. Perhaps not. We are all here to follow *our* life's path, not someone else's.

Another way we can help is to give of our time and energy. We can volunteer to help with fundraising and educational efforts to meet this crisis. We can send messages to our elected representatives in Congress that we want to allocate more of our resources to help those in the world who were not blessed to be born into a country that offers unprecedented opportunities for health, education, and employment.

I have highlighted world hunger in this lesson because it is a special concern of mine. There are, of course, many other worthy causes, some health-related and some not, for which you might develop compassion. For example, the HIV/AIDS virus, whose victims number 42 million world-wide as of December, 2002,[9] is certainly a global health crisis.

As I've said, living simply does not require you to give your time or money to those in need. I have found, however, from my own experiences and those of many others, a direct connection between living simply and the caring and compassionate side of ourselves. As we simplify our lives, caring about others feels more like a need and less like an obligation.

Life itself is the proper binge.

Julia Child

I was born in the United States to a middle class family due to luck, fate, or destiny. I could have been born to a life of poverty in a developing country. I am grateful for and enjoy the standard of living my birth circumstances have given me. If I had been born to a life of poverty, I would hope there would be someone like me out there who cared and who could help.

CONCLUSION

Bookstores and web sites are filled with advice on what and how much to eat, exercise, and rest. Information on other factors that affect our health, such as toxic substances in our environment, is also plentiful. Volumes have been written on the mind-body connection to health, herbal remedies, and natural supplements. Still, there is considerable controversy about how to enhance your health, especially when it comes to diet.

The field of health and well-being is far too vast to do it justice in this one lesson. Because of this fact and because of the wide range of conflicting opinions on health matters, I have refrained from providing a list of resources on health generally; any such list would be inadequate and would necessarily omit important resources.

What simplicity brings to the field of health is a lifestyle, a lifestyle that will give you the time, energy, and mindful presence to explore and implement healthy practices in your life.

Living simply, you will be motivated to do your own research and experimentation.

Education and compassion will lead us to care about others who have no realistic chance of enjoying good health. The ways we can help are limited only by our imaginations.

LESSON ASSIGNMENTS

FROM YOUR PERSONAL VIEWPOINT . . .

1. How would you rate your general level of health and well-being on a scale of 1 to 5, with 5 being excellent and 1 being very poor?
2. What are your general patterns of eating and drinking? Do you have a sense of how your body reacts to what you eat and drink? Explain any reactions you are aware of. Describe any changes you would like to make in your dietary habits.
3. How much sleep do you get? Do you feel it is enough? If not, what changes could you make in your life that would allow you to get sufficient sleep?
4. What is the role of exercise in your life? How much pleasure do you find in exercise? Is it integrated with other aspects of your life or is it something you do as a separate health practice? Think of possible forms of exercise opportunities you may have overlooked.
5. How would you describe your mental and emotional health? Is it what you want it to be? What factors contribute to your sense of well-being? What detracts from it? What can you do to improve this area of your life?
6. Are your health practices affected by those of your immediate family, friends, or housemates? If so, explain how.
7. Have you noticed changes in your health practices over the years? Do you feel that your interest in simplicity has affected your health in any way? If so, explain how.

Spirit and body differ not essentially, but gradually.

Anne Vicountess Conway

LOOKING AT THE BIGGER PICTURE . . .

8. Are there good sources for fresh, nutritious foods in your community? What are they?

9. Do you think the community you live in is very interested in healthful practices? Do the majority of people in your community engage in overall healthy living, or would you describe your area as health-challenged?
10. What are your feelings about world hunger? Does it seem real to you? Do you believe that there is anything we in North America can do about world hunger? If so, what? Are you personally willing to do anything?

LIFEWORK ASSIGNMENTS

Like any art, the creation of self is both natural and seemingly impossible.

Holly Near

1. Write down what you eat and drink for one week. Looking it over, were you surprised at the results? If you want to make changes, set small goals over gradual period of times. For example, if you want to reduce the amount of red meat in your diet, you might start with reducing portion size or frequency. If you quit altogether at one time, it may be more difficult to accomplish your goals.
2. Write an essay about your relationship to food. Describe the foods you love to eat—their taste, texture, and smell. What foods are comfort foods for you? Under what circumstances do you seek comfort foods? Talk about how foods feel in your stomach and body generally. Do some foods give you indigestion or stomach or intestinal pains?
3. Start an exercise program if you don't already have one. Be realistic. Do something you enjoy, and if it would help to do it with someone else, recruit a friend to join you. If you can't think of a single form of exercise you enjoy, try walking 10 minutes a day, slowly building up to 30 minutes a day. If you stick with it for a month or so, you are likely to start enjoying it. Most people do.
4. Consider giving your time or money to an organization committed to relieving hunger and improving the health of those who have insufficient resources in this area. If you decide to give money, consider using an automatic monthly credit card payment or bank account deduction. You are more likely to do it if it happens automatically.

ANNUAL CHECK-UP

1. Have there been any significant changes in your health or your health practices during the previous year? What are they?
2. Review the lifework assignments to see if you would like to start one or more projects.
3. What are your goals for your health for the coming year?

RECOMMENDED RESOURCES:

BOOKS

Better Basics for the Home: Simple Solutions for Less Toxic Living by Annie Berthold-Bond (New York: Three Rivers Press, 1999). Promotes the environmental and health benefits of a less toxic lifestyle. Offers more than 800 simple and practical alternatives to common household toxins, covering everything from skin care to gardening.

Diet for a New America: How Your Food Choices Affect Your Health, Happiness and the Future of Life on Earth by John Robbins (Novato, CA: H J Kramer, 1998). Fact-filled expose on the impact of America's meat and dairy agribusiness on our health and the health and well-being of the earth and its creatures. Advocates elimination or at least a reduction of meat and animal products in the diet.

The Food Revolution: How Your Diet Can Help Save Your Life and Our World by John Robbins (Berkeley, CA: Conari Press, 2001). Sequel to bestselling book, *Diet for a New America*, this book explores impacts of various diets and their attendant food manufacturing practices on personal health, the treatment of animals, and the sustainability of the earth. Reviews a broad range of subjects, including global hunger and genetic engineering.

Hope's Edge: The Next Diet for a Small Planet by Frances Moore Lappé and Anna Lappé (New York: J.P. Tarcher, 2002). Sequel to bestselling book, *Diet for a Small Planet*, published thirty years earlier, Frances Moore Lappé and her daughter present arguments for a vegetarian diet in the context of personal health, the world economy, and global hunger. Includes stories from the authors' journey around the world where they discovered many examples of people using organic, food producing alternatives.

MISCELLANEOUS

Doctors Without Borders [www.doctorswithoutborders.org] is an international, volunteer-based organization that provides both emergency aid to victims of armed conflict, epidemics, and natural and man-made disasters and on-going health care to those who lack health care due to social or geographical isolation.

JustGive [www.justgive.org] maintains an extensive database of charitable organizations in a wide range of categories, including health and disease, hunger and poverty, and the environment.

NOTE: *Additions and updates to these resources can be found on The Simplicity Resource Guide at www.gallagherpress.com/pierce.*

LESSON 10

FINDING JOY IN FRIENDS AND FAMILY

RELATIONSHIPS AND SIMPLICITY

Most people value personal relationships over work and wealth. But we often forget this fact until and unless we lose someone dear or come close to losing someone. Or until we ourselves become seriously ill or injured. Then, it all becomes crystal clear. The people we love are more important to us than anything else.

How unfortunate it is that we so often lose sight of this truth! However, when we are preoccupied with the day-to-day demands of a rushed and harried lifestyle, it's easy to lose track of what's most important.

Quality relationships require at least two ingredients: time and a certain level of attention, which could be described as mindful interaction. If you feel stressed or overwhelmed in your job, you may (or may not) have enough time with your loved ones, but it's unlikely you'll have the presence of mind to interact with them in meaningful ways. It is difficult to be really present at such times. Part of your mind is back on the job.

Living simply creates an environment where quality relationships can flourish. With reasonable working hours and less stress in your life, there is room for more spontaneity and joy with others. You will have the capacity to give more of yourself and receive more from your loved ones.

I spent a great deal of time supporting my parents during the last years of my father's life, when his health was poor. My siblings often expressed appreciation, and sometimes guilt, related to this support. But I felt fortunate because, while there were difficult challenges and stressful times, it was deeply satisfying to help my parents at this critical stage of their lives. Living more simply enabled me to give them time, which I would otherwise be spending at work. I am very grateful for that opportunity.

Living simply almost always enhances personal relationships. Here are some comments from people in my simplicity study:

> All of the serious relationships with family and close friends have become stronger and deeper. I speculate that this is be-

cause my attention to the meaning of life, which precipitated my voluntary simplicity, logically brought me to devote more life energy to relationships. By dumping those activities that seemed of low value, I've had both more time and a heightened sense of the value of maintaining strong connections with other people.

Recently, one of my cousins called and asked if I would photograph my Aunt and Uncle's 50th wedding anniversary party. If I had still been working my full-time job, it would have been nearly impossible for me to do this. As it turned out, not only did I photograph the celebration, I took portraits of all my relatives who attended the celebration. I was able to create a one-day family album of my large extended family—several hundred pictures that to me (and my relatives) are priceless. Simplifying has not meant that we are living "less." In fact we feel richer. I feel like I can put my arms around the experiences and time that are of great importance to us.

Joy is the holy fire that keeps our purpose warm and our intelligence aglow.

Helen Keller

NOTHING SIMPLE ABOUT CHILDREN

Marie Sherlock opens her book, *Living Simply with Children*, by announcing that for most American families, living simply with children is the ultimate oxymoron. Parents are working more hours than ever while children have substantially increased time spent on sports (both participatory and spectator) and studying.[1] In fact, national surveys show that children lost 12 hours of free time per week from 1981 to 1997, including a 50 percent drop in unstructured outdoor activities.[2] Only one-third of American families have dinner together on a daily basis.[3]

As parents, we want the best for our children. But we have evolved into a society of people who work long hours, drive great distances to work, and maintain large homes and lots, resulting in less unstructured time to spend with our children. In some instances, we try to compensate for that by giving our kids more material things and every opportunity to participate in whatever stimulating activities our schools, churches, and civic organizations come up with. Also, since we're not always able to be home with our children, we feel it's better for them to be engaged in structured, supervised activities—sports, music, arts, church activities, and endless other choices—rather than roaming the streets or sitting at home bored.

This is not to say that extra curricular activities are not highly valuable to children. They are. But we have taken a good thing and erroneously concluded that more is better. As a result, we see many sleep-deprived families who become increasingly dependent on external stimulation. We have lost the ability to just hang out—to while away a Sunday afternoon with absolutely no plans. We can hardly imagine spending a day as a family making it up as we go along—deciding what to do, when to eat, spontaneously and as the spirit moves us.

Fortunately the family is a human institution: humans made it and humans can change it.

Shere Hite

The key to living simply with children, as with all other aspects of simplicity, is balance, which of course is *much* easier said than done. In addition to freeing up time to parent our children, we need to resist the social pressures all around us to grant our kids every new opportunity that beckons.

Fortunately, there is abundant help and support, including some great books and organizations committed to helping families regain balance (see Recommended Resources at the end of this lesson).

Parents use a variety of tools to integrate the principles of simplicity with family life. Some parents carefully monitor the television watched by their children to minimize exposure to commercial messages, violence, and inappropriate programming. Educating children—even as young as three years old—about the trade-offs between more stuff or more quality time together can be effective. Some families involve their older children in the family budgeting process with great success. This first-hand experience with the family budget helps children learn to distinguish between needs and wants.

Limiting the number of extra curricular activities of *both* parents and children is essential to achieve balance. It's hard for a parent to persuade a child to limit outside activities if the parent's activity level is out of control.

In their book, *Putting Family First*, William J. Doherty and Barbara Z. Carlson stress the importance of conversation and connection within the family. Family rituals such as eating dinner together, sharing a bedtime story, or playing catch in the front yard establish the foundation for the real event—communicating and connecting with each other. These rituals become a safe place for laughter, feelings, and concerns about the world to be expressed and welcomed with love.

I remember a childhood ritual I shared with my mother. The first thing I did when I walked in the door from school—back in the dark ages when children walked or rode their bicycles to school—was to find my mother, who, as the mother of eight children, was usually folding laundry. I would talk to her non-stop for 20 minutes or so about everything that happened in my day. She listened intently, and when I finished I felt grounded again in my family. I really wasn't *home* until I had that talk with my mom.

Love is what's left when you let go of everything you don't need.

Erich Schiffmann

GIFTS OF LOVE

Sharing gifts with loved ones is an important ritual. The giving of a gift brings something intangible—the feeling of love—to life. Gifts come in many sizes and shapes. If corporations ruled the world, we would communicate our love with frequent gifts of material goods—the stronger our love, the more expensive the gift. For example, a diamond ring is considered by some to be the ultimate expression of a man's love for a woman.

But corporations don't rule the world—not completely, anyway. People who live simply do not limit themselves to material gifts, but are much more imaginative in their gift choices. They favor gifts of the heart over gifts of the wallet.

Like most couples, my husband and I started out exchanging gifts at Christmas and treating each other to birthday treasures. As our earnings grew, so did our gifts, both in number and in value. Clothes, jewelry, and electronic toys were our favorites. However, after a number of years together, selecting gifts became more of a challenge. We already had enough of most things. It became more difficult to guess what the other might enjoy. We frequently returned items to the store because they weren't quite right. Finally, we looked at each other and said, "Let's not do this anymore." We decided to find another way to celebrate our love and the milestones in our lives.

For over 10 years now, we have given each other experiences rather than material gifts. One especially warm Christmas day, we bought ourselves a nice bottle of wine, put together a gourmet picnic, and spent the afternoon on a beach on the Big Sur coast. For a recent birthday, my husband drove me to San Francisco (a few hours drive) to a museum I had been eager to visit, followed by a lunch in an outdoor restaurant overlooking a park. A perfect gift.

Nevertheless, material gifts can be just as special when they are truly valued by the recipient. It's very rewarding to buy or make something we know our loved one will cherish. But too often we struggle to come up with gift ideas for holidays and birthdays. Sometimes, it's a burden.

Friendship is the bread of the heart.

Mary Russell Mitford

There are simple ways to bring more joy to the gift giving experience. Here are just a few possibilities:

- Material gifts. Don't wait until two weeks before an event to buy a gift. If you enjoy giving material gifts, be thinking of your loved ones throughout the year and purchase gifts when you come across just the right item.
- Gifts of your labor. You could offer to babysit once a week to allow your loved one to take a class he or she is interested in. Helping a friend plant a spring garden or preparing a special meal for someone are wonderful gifts.
- Gifts of shared events. Plan a special outing for you and your loved one to enjoy together. A hike and a picnic, a day exploring back country roads or a small town you haven't visited before, or an evening of theater are just a few ideas. Think of something unusual that your loved one would enjoy.
- Gifts of dreams. What does your loved one dream about? Is there some adventure or creative pursuit that beckons to her? If he yearns to take great photographs, give him the gift of a photography class. If she enjoys being in nature, how about a kayaking excursion?
- Gifts of giving. Some families decide to give to others rather than to each other during special holidays. Helping to prepare a community Thanksgiving dinner or sponsoring a family at Christmas by offering food and presents can be very satisfying.

SPOUSES AND SIGNIFICANT OTHERS

Of course, living simply in itself does not guarantee happiness. For example, if you want to simplify your life and your spouse or significant other does not, tension and stress are likely to result. It is not uncommon for one person in a marriage or primary relationship to want to simplify to a greater degree or sooner than the other. This can be especially challenging if the anticipated lifestyles changes are dramatic.

If you want to simplify and your spouse is reluctant, consider using the "but-it's-in-your-best-interest-sweetie" technique. Figure out what your spouse truly desires in life and then show him that simplicity can help him get it. This method worked fairly well with my husband. I prepared a spreadsheet—he relates best to things he can count—showing him how much sooner we could reach financial independence if we reduced our housing expenses. Even though he enjoys his work as a real estate agent, and would likely continue working part-time even if we didn't need to work for a living, he would also love the freedom that comes with financial independence. This realization made him feel more positive about selling our large home and downscaling.

Few are the giants of the soul who actually feel that the human race is their family circle.

Elizabeth Wray Taylor

It's important to remember that there is no place for a holier-than-thou attitude when choosing a simple way of life. In the end, if your primary relationship is a good one, notwithstanding your different views on simplicity, it may come down to accepting your mate as he or she is. Here is one woman's story taken from my book, *Choosing Simplicity*:

> I drive a 12-year-old car, wear mostly garage-sale clothes, and generally try to avoid excessive consumerism. My husband loves cars and other big-ticket items. This led to serious conflict in the past, but we've now learned to peacefully co-exist; he has scaled down his wants quite a bit, and I've become less judgmental of his habits. I've realized that even though he's more materialistic than I am, he's still far less preoccupied with things than most Americans.
>
> My husband and I continue to learn from each other, although I think he's probably changed more than I have. Things are about to get even more interesting, because we're expect-

> ing our first child in October. I'm pretty much a tofu girl, and my hubby is still a McDonald's boy . . . I really have no idea what that kid is going to end up eating!

It's best to approach conflicts about simplicity as you would any other relationship conflict. Open communication, lack of judgment about the other's preferences, compromise, and patience are all effective tools for reconciling your differences. Even if your spouse does not share your simplicity values, there is a great deal you can do individually to live simply. You still have some control over how you spend *your* time, energy, and money.

> *Having someone wonder where you are when you don't come home at night is a very old human need.*
>
> Margaret Mead

FRIENDSHIPS

A similar conflict may arise in relationships with friends. Sometimes when a person simplifies his or her life, the basis for friendship with certain others may fall away. For example, if the primary focus of a friendship is shopping together, there must be more to that friendship or it will probably disappear. One woman describes her experience:

> I am no longer close with women who work full-time, have huge new homes, wear the latest fashions, drive several new vehicles, have their kids in daycare, and complain they have no time or money. I seek out women who enjoy raising their families, gardening, browsing at rummage sales, sewing and crafting, baking from scratch, etc.

It can also be frustrating if your lifestyle has changed but there are few others to share it with, as described by one person:

> If we have had one disappointment (for lack of a better word) with our decision to simplify, it has been that we still find it hard to develop good relationships with people. We may have simplified, but others are still so busy and overcommitted. We know that we value time with people more than accumulating more stuff, but they are still super busy buying for their chil-

> dren. We have found that people we know talk about simplifying, but when it comes down to making the hard choices and actually letting go of things and activities, they don't seem to be able to do it. So we have a lot more time, but still find it hard to get together with people because they are so busy every night. It is unbelievable.

Over time, you may let some friendships go and take on new ones. Keep in mind that we don't *have* friends, as in owning something, but rather we *experience* moments of friendship. In some cases, those moments of friendship can last for decades. In letting go of a friendship, we haven't lost a friend; we are simply allowing those particular moments of friendship to pass.

One can never consent to creep when one feels an impulse to soar.

Helen Keller

We've talked about letting go of excess possessions and clutter to free ourselves. Similarly, sometimes we need to let go of certain relationships—those that drain our energy and bring us down. It's wise to avoid spending time with negative people who find little right with this world and love to hear themselves whine. Or people who offer you no support, only criticism.

This can be especially challenging if you are related to the negative people in your life. Sharing a gene pool doesn't mean you have to like a relative or spend a great deal of time with him or her. Of course, we need to balance those feelings with obligations to care for our children, our parents, and sometimes other relatives.

When you let go of relationships that no longer nurture you, you have more time and energy to invest in those that do. The relationships that remain will generally grow stronger, deeper, and more satisfying.

CONCLUSION

Enhanced relationships with friends and family are the sweetest benefits of living simply. With simplicity, we structure our lives to bring this high priority into its rightful place. It is not always an easy and smooth ride, but the rewards are substantial.

LESSON ASSIGNMENTS

FROM YOUR PERSONAL VIEWPOINT . . .

1. Think back to your childhood. Describe one or more of your favorite memories? How significant were people in those memories?
2. On a scale of 1 to 5, with 5 being the highest, what value would you assign to personal relationships? (Note: this is not a question about the quality of your current relationships but about how much you generally value relationships.) Do you feel that you have enough time and energy to devote to your relationships?
3. Other than your family, how many close friends are there in your life? Do you feel that this number is too low, too high, or just right? Do you need to de-clutter your friendship closet? If so, which relationships are you ready to let go of? How might you go about this?
4. What sorts of gifts do you give to the people you love? Does gift selection and buying feel like a chore or is it a source of joy for you? Generally, do your gifts offer the recipient something that is needed or cherished? If not, what would be some alternatives?
5. What shared activities would enhance your relationships with your loved ones? Don't limit yourself to activities in the usual sense. Snuggling up on the couch to share what happened in your day counts, too. Are there ways you can incorporate more of these activities into your life?
6. Do you feel that your interest in simplicity has caused tension in your relationships with loved ones? If so, what creative actions or mental adjustments could relieve that tension? As your values shift toward a simpler way of life, do you anticipate losing interest in some relationships?
7. How much time do you spend with people whom you would rather not see but do so out of habit or because you don't know how to say no. Be honest. Think of creative ways of saying no to those with whom you don't

Intimate relationships cannot substitute for a life plan. But to have any meaning or viability at all, a life plan must include intimate relationships.

Harriet Lerner

have a family or work-related obligation. Telling someone you cannot get together because you have another commitment is not a lie, even if you spend that time reading a book in front of the fire. You *do* have another commitment—a commitment to yourself to live an authentic and balanced life.

8. Are there people in your life with whom you would like to be closer? What are some ways you could spend more time with them?
9. If you have children at home, how important are material things to them? What would be some creative ways to teach them to value nonmaterial aspects of life? How much TV do they watch? What percentage of it is noncommercial TV?
10. If you have children at home, how balanced are their lives? How much unstructured play time do they enjoy each week (not including watching television, surfing the Internet, or playing video games)? How much one-on-one time do you have with each child? How important are each of their extra curricular activities? If you feel their activity level is too high, which activities would be best to phase out?

Human relations just are not fixed in their orbits like the planets—they're more like galaxies, changing all the time, exploding into light for years, then dying away.

May Sarton

LOOKING AT THE BIGGER PICTURE . . .

11. How do the institutions in your life—schools, churches, employers, neighborhoods, and other groups—help or hinder your ability to connect and share with your loved ones?
12. Describe any social and public policies that would help to strengthen relationships among friends and families?

LIFEWORK ASSIGNMENTS

1. If you live with others, have a meeting with your family or roommates to talk about how you are doing. Encourage each person to voice his hopes and expectations about your relationships, including a limited time (10 minutes or so) for griping. Then, as a family or group who share a home, think of ways to enhance your relationships. Per-

haps there are rituals, such as a family meal, you can integrate into your daily or weekly routines.

2. Set some relationship goals for the coming year. What, if anything, do you want to change? Come up with a plan to accomplish your objectives. For example, if you want to spend more time with your spouse, decide on a ritual—perhaps setting aside a special time each day or a longer time during the week to be together.
3. If you would like to explore giving nonmaterial gifts to your loved ones, talk to them about your ideas. See what their interests are. If you are going to change your gift patterns, it's best to let your loved ones know ahead of time so they don't misconstrue your intentions. Use this opportunity to express your positive thoughts and feelings about them so that this change becomes a welcome part of your relationship.

A relationship isn't meant to be an insurance policy, a life preserver or a security blanket.

Diane Crowley

ANNUAL CHECK-UP

1. Review questions # 1 through 10 of the lesson assignments. Have your relationships changed during the last year? If so, describe the changes. Are you pleased with the results?
2. Set some relationship goals for the following year. Come up with detailed plans on how to accomplish your objectives.

RECOMMENDED RESOURCES

BOOKS

Living Simply With Children: A Voluntary Simplicity Guide by Marie Sherlock (New York: Three Rivers Press, 2003). Comprehensive book about the challenges of living simply with children, including finding more time to be with your kids, dealing with your child's peer pressures to want more stuff, and teaching your children to care about the earth.

The Paradox of Natural Mothering by Chris Bobel (Philadelphia: Temple University Press, 2001). Sociologist examines feminist and other paradoxes of natural mothering, which can be defined by its preferences for home birthing, extended breast feeding, home schooling, and natural health care. Voluntary simplicity and attachment parenting are frequently practiced by natural mothers.

Putting Family First: Successful Strategies for Reclaiming Family Life in a Hurry-Up World by William Doherty and Barbara Carlson (New York: Owl Books, 2002). Founders of family advocacy organization present guide to restore balance in family life. They offer tips for establishing family rituals, such as a shared family meal, to enhance communication and connection within the family.

Raising Kids with Just a Little Cash by Lisa Reid (Santa Fe, NM: Ferguson-Carol Publishers, 1996). Book packed with practical advice on how to save money when it comes to kids—on clothing, toys, entertainment, education, birthdays, food, health, travel, and holidays.

Simple Living: One Couple's Search for a Better Life by Frank Levering and Wanda Urbanska (New York: Viking Penguin, 1992). Memoir of a couple's journey to simplify their lives—from a life as struggling writers in Los Angeles to working partners in an family-owned orchard business in Virginia.

Simple Loving: A Path to Deeper, More Sustainable Relationships by Janet Luhrs (New York: Penguin USA, 2000). Sourcebook to show readers how to apply the principles of simplicity to develop deeper, more passionate, and more loving relationships. Includes inspirational quotes, effective relationship practices, and recommended resources.

Simplify Your Life with Kids: 100 Ways to Make Family Life Easier and More Fun by Elaine St. James (Kansas City, MO: Andrews McMeel Publishing, 2000). A practical guide for working parents, this book offers tips and suggestions on the specific challenges of parenthood.

Unplug the Christmas Machine: A Complete Guide to Putting Love and Joy Back into the Season by Jo Robinson and Jean Coppock Staeheli (New York: Quill, Revised 1991). Explores how to create a more meaningful holiday, focusing on deeply satisfying spiritual and family experiences, rather than engaging in excessive materialism.

What Kids Really Want That Money Can't Buy by Betsy Taylor (New York: Warner Books, 2003). Co-founder of the *Center for the*

New American Dream offers practical advice on how parents can give their kids what matters most: time, love, and attention. Includes first-person accounts from parents and children.

MISCELLANEOUS

Putting Family First [www.familylife1st.org] is a grass-roots movement for building communities where family life is honored and celebrated. This organization helps parents work with each other, as well as with schools, churches, neighborhoods, and other community organizations, to develop policies that support family life.

WorkingMomMall.com [www.workingmommall.com] was developed by working moms as a resource for busy, working moms to maintain balance in their lives. In addition to a comprehensive website filled with relevant news, articles, tips, and related links, it offers a newsletter and an on-line discussion group.

NOTE: *Additions and updates to these resources can be found on The Simplicity Resource Guide at www.gallagherpress.com/pierce.*

LESSON 11

EMBRACING COMMUNITY

WHAT IS COMMUNITY?

My husband and I recently visited Italy, renting apartments for one week each in four different cities. Our favorite was the small town of Lucca in Tuscany. This largely traffic-free town favors pedestrians and bicyclists who occupy the full width of the streets, only moving over to let an occasional car pass. The town is surrounded by a large 17th century wall—three miles in circumference and many meters wide—that has been turned into a park with areas for walking, bicycling, picnicking, and just lolling about. You can get everything you need (from food to furniture) within the town limits.

As is typical in Italian towns, many piazzas (plazas), large and small, were scattered throughout Lucca. In the evenings, we would often hang out at Piazza Napoleone, located just a few blocks from our apartment, while consuming our daily gelato (or in some cases our second gelato of the day). There, people of all ages gathered to play, talk, and to share their days and good cheer. Young children ran from one end of the wide piazza to the other while adults sat and visited at tables surrounding the piazza. Teenagers grouped, huddled together to share intimate secrets, then regrouped to expand on the stories and intrigue of their lives. Couples strolled hand in hand.

My impression is that this piazza, indeed the entire town, belongs to everyone. The town is an extension of individual homes and apartments. The townspeople are an extension of individual families. They live in splendid community.

It is this vision of community that propels the growth of livable towns and cities in North America (see Lesson 4 for a discussion of this trend). We need the physical infrastructure—attractive public spaces, pedestrian and bicycle paths, and higher density housing—to facilitate connecting with our neighbors. We need to make our neighborhoods and towns an extension of our living rooms.

Undoubtedly, the experience of community in North America—the sharing and interdependence of people living in the same neighborhood or town—has decreased substantially in the last 50 years. For one thing, our standard of living has doubled during that period and we can now afford to buy most things we need, rather than having to borrow or exchange items with neighbors. When one-car families were the norm, people carpooled more. Our homes, now doubled in size, are electronic showcases, giving us fewer reasons to seek entertainment outside our own walls. Believing that continual economic growth is essential—otherwise our economy would collapse, so say advocates of growth—businesses encourage people to purchase whatever they need or want rather than share goods with others.

A community can never be created: not through hard work or in any other way. It must simply be recognized and respected.

Sigrid Nielsen

Community means more than the interdependence of people for their basic needs. It also implies sharing and trusting on other levels: emotional, intellectual, spiritual, and recreational. You can experience community in many settings—an adult education class, a pot-luck dinner, a church service, a neighborhood softball game, or in an informal conversation at a local coffee house. Even one-on-one friendships are a form of community.

The experience of community can also extend beyond our immediate geographical area to statewide, national, and global arenas. With the advances of the Internet and email, people routinely share information, give and receive support, and work on common causes with others the world over.

While the Internet has the potential to enhance community, it's not without its critics. Some are concerned that the Internet, like television, can inhibit community by encouraging people to spend long hours absorbed in solitary entertainment. On the other hand, virtual community sharing occurs in the form of email correspondence, online discussion groups, and educational programs. The Internet also allows us to communicate more easily with people from other countries, which may prove to play a critical role in global peace. The better we clearly comprehend what others in the world are experiencing, the more likely it is that we will act with compassion and understanding.

In my simplicity study, I asked people to describe their experiences of community. Many mentioned their involvement (or lack thereof) in structured forms of community, such as volunteer work or participation in civic activities. Only 26 percent of the study participants were actively involved in such community efforts. Many who were not expressed regret, disappointment, or guilt that they were not more involved. Here are some of their comments:

> This [community involvement] is one of our goals that we have yet to reach. We both long for a sense of community, but find that it is difficult to fit in after work, family, and us as a couple.

> I am not involved in my community as much as I would like to be. I live in a very large community that is culturally, economically, and socially diverse. My community is relatively safe, though many surrounding communities are infested with crime, gangs, ignorance, and violence, which deeply concerns me. I would love to work with people of all ages, cultures, and religious affiliations. I suffer from major guilt in this area, because I have not yet made the effort to participate in my community the way my intuition tells me I could.

Never fear shadows. They simply mean there's a light shining somewhere nearby.

Ruth E. Renkel

Some people make a conscious choice not to get involved in organized community activities because of the frustrations inherent in working with an organization. As one study participant explained:

> I'm finding collective action to be increasingly frustrating and de-energizing. This is the case because we are still awaiting the emergence of effective alternative forms of organizing and guiding collective human activities. In my part of the world, whenever people clump together to work toward a common purpose, they invariably default to traditional institutional and organizational forms (corporations, by-laws, boards of directors, committees, hierarchies, and politics). Inherent in these very forms are all the shortcomings that are rendering life on earth unsustainable, and all their destructive gambits are played out over and over. We need fundamentally new organizational forms if we're going to achieve fundamentally positive social goals.

Others feel that they don't have time for community involvement and don't feel guilty about it either. As one woman explained:

> We are not involved that much with community activities—mainly our neighbors and family. We look out for one another, but as far as being a part of civic organizations, we aren't. I want my family to enjoy our lives; outside interests usually mean running around a lot on evenings or weekends. I figure after a hard day at work and school, the best thing we can do is enjoy each other and not have to push ourselves. I want my kids to remember being a kid—not a clock watcher.

Non-doing means letting things be and allowing them to unfold in their own way.

Jon Kabat-Zinn

Initially, I was surprised that only a relatively small percentage of people in the study were actively involved in their communities. Later I realized that I, like many of the study participants, had a concept of community that was far too narrow. We all thought of community strictly in terms of traditional, organized forms, such as food coops, parent-teacher associations, local politics, and organized volunteer work. Because many lacked the interest or time to participate in such organized activities, they often expressed regret or guilt.

However, some of the most rewarding community experiences occur outside this realm. Like the nightly piazza gatherings in Lucca, we experience community whenever we spend time sharing and caring for family, neighbors, and friends. Based on this broader view, the vast majority of the study participants experienced a great deal of community in their lives. There were many instances of people sharing skills and resources with others—helping a neighbor plant a garden, exchanging childcare duties, lending tools to friends. For many of them, community was integrated with the rest of their lives, not something they did as a distinct activity separate from work, family, and the business of living.

DOES SELF-SUFFICIENCY INHIBIT COMMUNITY?

The relationship between community and simplicity is an interesting one, at times ambiguous and paradoxical. On one hand, some people who live simply take great pride and pleasure in being self-sufficient, doing things like repairing their own automobiles, growing their own food, or making their own clothes. These people reduce their monetary needs by doing for themselves what they would otherwise pay others to do. This lifestyle is in tune with the rugged, individualistic character of North American culture.

Usefulness, whatever form it may take, is the price we should pay for the air we breathe and the food we eat and the privilege of being alive.

Eleanor Roosevelt

On the other hand, the experience of community is often heralded as a desirable, if not essential, element of living simply. This begs the question: Is the objective to be as self-sufficient as possible, decreasing one's dependence on others, or should we work toward a model of living that emphasizes community and interdependence? The answer is neither and both.

The question of self-sufficiency is primarily one of personal style and preference. Some people derive considerable satisfaction from activities such as cooking, gardening, or working on home remodeling projects. They talk about the pleasures of creative expression, working with their hands, and feeling a sense of accomplishment. For some, reducing the income they need to live on is the primary benefit of these activities. For others, saving money by being self-sufficient is a bonus to an otherwise fulfilling activity.

Then there are those for whom self-sufficiency is an illusive dream. I, for one, can barely operate a VCR (how did it happen that we now need about four remote controls to operate a simple television?), much less cook edible meals from scratch (not that I haven't tried). So the value of self-sufficiency is relative to a person's interests and skills. Don't forget: simplicity is not about deprivation. It's important to be conscious of the reasons you want to develop self-sufficiency in a given area. To the extent that you derive inherent satisfaction from the task in addition to saving money, so much the better.

Let's assume you enjoy doing for yourself and reaping the benefits of living on less. What does that mean in terms of community? It is possible to be both highly self-sufficient and interdependent with others. For example, Joe may be great at repairing his own car, but his neighbor cuts his hair in exchange for produce from Joe's garden. Perhaps an ideal community would consist of highly self-sufficient individuals who share their proficiency in the living arts with each other.

WORKING AND PLAYING TOGETHER

Call it a clan, call it a network, call it a tribe, call it a family. Whatever you call it, whoever you are, you need one.

Jane Howard

There are ways to experience community without adding to our responsibilities and chores. For example, one couple I know lives in a small downtown apartment without a washer and dryer. Every other Saturday they join similarly-situated friends for a morning at the laundromat, catching up on each other's lives, laughing at each other's jokes, and enjoying each other's company. While their clothes are drying, they go next door to a café to enjoy a pancake breakfast.

When working with others, chores feel less like drudgery and more like a party. You can hear this in the laughter and see it in the smiles of some people who live in traditional societies in developing countries. How can they be having so much fun? Their bodies may be doing mundane chores, but their hearts and spirits are having a blast.

We, too, can combine work with play. For example, several households could team up for major projects, spending a weekend day once a month at a different home, painting a bedroom, cleaning out the gutters, or planting a garden. By simply joining others in the activities of daily living—presto, we have community.

Working with others adds not only pleasure but also meaning to our activities. For example, people who work on Habitat for Humanity projects, natural disaster relief programs, and charity fund-raising events talk about the bonds they feel with their co-workers in toiling for a common good.

Playing together also builds community. In North America, we have lost the joy of daily, spontaneous singing. Cecile Andrews, author of *Circle of Simplicity*, has been known to break up simplicity seminars by asking everyone to stand up and sing, *You Are My Sunshine*. The first time I saw her do this, I thought,

"Wait, Cecile, are you nuts? These people don't want to sing some dumb song. They're here to learn about simplicity." But, in fact, they did and do—we all want to make music and sing songs, especially those we know the words to. We all enjoyed singing as children but as we developed self-consciousness in adolescence, the singing stopped.

Singing and dancing are voices of the spirit. We should let our spirits speak. The fact that I can't carry a tune doesn't stop me from singing around the house even though I sometimes acquiesce to my husband's pleas to stop.

I enjoy a special community experience every Wednesday when I join a small group of other middle-aged women (except for one 50-something beauty who thinks she's 30) for a 6 to 10 mile hike in the Big Sur mountains near my home. We take in the spectacular beauty while talking, laughing, and righting the wrongs of the world. We've been doing this for three years and I expect we will continue into our 80's. We variously call ourselves the *Glamazons* or *Babes in the Woods* or during the tick season, *Chicks with Ticks*.

> *Laughter is the lightning rod of play, the eroticism of conversation.*
>
> Eva Hoffman

LEARNING TOGETHER

If you are working with this book as part of a simplicity study group, you are witnessing learning in community first-hand. Sharing the learning process with others can be very empowering, stimulating, and fruitful. I'm always impressed with how much dynamic learning takes place in simplicity workshops. We are in fact all students and teachers of each other.

For centuries, people have met in groups of all sizes and shapes to discuss everything under the sun. In addition to formal educational programs, town meetings, knitting circles, and casual gatherings in market squares have all provided opportunities for learning together.

What intrigues me is the potential for learning in unstructured, spontaneous settings. For example, I have experienced and heard others say that some of the most valuable learning experiences at conferences are the informal group conversations that take place in between the structured sessions.

Another example of a powerful, informal learning process

Adventure can be an end in itself. Self-discovery is the secret ingredient that fuels daring.

Grace Lichtenstein

can be found in the emerging movement of Conversation Cafés, launched in Seattle by Vicki Robin, social activist and coauthor of *Your Money or Your Life*, in 2001. At Conversation Cafés, friends, neighbors, and strangers gather in a public setting, usually a café, to share food or drink and talk about the important things in life. These conversations typically last about 90 minutes and are facilitated by a host. The topic is either pre-selected by the host or decided by the group on the spot. The range of topics is quite broad—everything from the impact of September 11th to concerns about the quality of our children's education. Rules are few, the most important of which is to allow each person an opportunity (but without obligation) to share his views. No preparation or specific knowledge is required. No actions are planned or committees formed. It's all about talking and sharing—the magic of conversation.

Conversation Cafés represent community in action in its simplest form. There are no by-laws, membership dues, or squabbles about who is not doing their fair share of the work. There is no work, at least on an outer level. In fact, there is considerable inner work taking place. In sharing their concerns and views about life, participants learn who they really are inside. And they experience an intimate connection with people whom they may have just met. Conversation Cafés have the potential to launch a cultural revolution, breaking down the walls of isolation in our culture. If you would like to participate in a Conversation Café, log on to www.conversationcafe.org for further information.

LIVING TOGETHER

Living with others beyond your immediate family, while not for everyone, offers many benefits and can be found in any number of innovative living arrangements. The primary benefit of these alternatives is to experience community informally as a part of daily life. In many though not all instances, it may also be less expensive to live in some form of cohousing or intentional community. It is worth considering as we work at ways to live more simply.

A cohousing community typically consists of a group of

COMMUNE

people who pool resources to purchase land, build individual and group housing spaces, and live as a community, sharing some meals and often many resources. Developing a cohousing community can be a labor intensive process, but for many, the rewards are substantial. Each family typically purchases its own self-sufficient dwelling as well as an interest in the common facilities. The Recommended Resources at the end of this lesson will give you more information on cohousing communities.

There are many less formal models of shared housing. For example, owners of units in condominium (or co-op) projects share walls, landscaping, garages, and often laundry facilities. Sometimes, condominium owners will share a vegetable garden, childcare, or occasional group parties. Condominium living may or may not provide the community interaction of a more traditional cohousing environment, but at a minimum, it conserves natural resources.

When you hug someone, you learn something else about them. An important something else.

E.L. Konigsburg

Another model of shared housing occurs when a small group of people—perhaps four to six—rent or buy a home together. This is commonly done by college students but there's no reason why people of all ages can't do it. It might be especially rewarding for single seniors who have the physical and mental health to live independently. A creative real estate lawyer can draft an agreement in a purchase situation to provide for the interests of each person and what would happen in the event that someone passes away or moves on.

Other age groups that would benefit from this arrangement include young people in their 20's just starting out on their own. In addition to the social benefits of companionship, there are potential cost savings on furniture, appliances, and entertainment gadgets, all of which, if purchased individually, can saddle young people with major debt by the time they are 30. Carpooling and sharing automobiles may also be possible, saving both money and the earth's resources. One person in my simplicity study, a dentist, lived in this manner during his twenties and thirties. By the time he reached 40, he was financially independent. Since then, he has been traveling the world, occasionally working or volunteering as a dentist.

You need not be limited to single-family homes to create a

shared housing environment. Other structures—warehouse lofts, apartment buildings, or an old motel—may provide excellent, less expensive ways to live well with others.

A NEW LOOK AT SENIOR RESIDENCE COMMUNITIES

Senior residence communities provide models of cohousing that could be used for other age groups. For example, let's consider a typical senior community for independent living—one that offers individual living residences (apartments and/or cottages) together with shared spaces for meals, lounges, exercise rooms, a library, a computer room, and project/hobby rooms. Local transportation and entertainment activities—both on and off-site—are often included in this type of senior project.

No sooner do we think we have assembled a comfortable life than we find a piece of ourselves that has no place to fit in.

Gail Sheehy

Older people often move into a senior residence community when they tire of home maintenance and food preparation or need extra support services such as transportation. However, the downside to these communities was aptly expressed by my 80-year-old mother when she moved out of a senior community saying, "I don't like living with a bunch of old people." In North America, we segregate our elders, to the detriment of all.

Why limit such communities to seniors? Combining all age groups would provide a richer, more diversified experience for all. There could be safe, enclosed, inside and outdoor areas for kids to play with separate, quiet common areas for those who prefer a more peaceful environment. Some older residents would thoroughly enjoy the presence of children, and younger people would benefit from interacting with the wisdom holders of society. Parents could easily exchange childcare services. Workers could carpool. Teenagers could teach older residents how to operate a computer. Single people need not be lonely. People would still have their independent living space for private time. Residents could easily share and exchange possessions. Bartering for services would also be feasible.

Depending on the age, abilities, and interests of the residents, each person or family could contribute money, labor, or a combination of both to support the community. Companies similar to those that now operate senior residences could manage these communities. In contrast to a traditional cohousing development, residency could be offered on a rental basis, eliminating the risk of investing in a venture you may not be sure about.

Of course, while some people thrive on this level of community interaction, there are natural loners who would not like it one bit. It is not possible or desirable to provide one housing model for everyone. Like livable towns and cities, this is just another alternative to live in community while maintaining some degree of independence and autonomy.

To the extent that we share the art of living with others, we will feel a greater sense of purpose and less isolation in our lives. If we ask and expect our local governmental representatives to create the infrastructure to develop these and other creative alternatives, it will happen. If there is sufficient demand, it will also work economically.

If one is out of touch with oneself, then one cannot touch others.

Anne Morrow Lindbergh

CONCLUSION

As you can see, the experience of community comes in many shapes and variations. Unfortunately, community is often sacrificed when our lives are out of balance. If we work excessively, community is not likely to be a high priority in our lives. We are not likely to want to connect with others if we are exhausted or stressed out. Participating in community should always be something you do to experience life more fully, and not simply to avoid feelings of guilt. We have enough *shoulds* in our lives; we don't need to add community to that list.

LESSON ASSIGNMENTS

FROM YOUR PERSONAL VIEWPOINT . . .

1. When you think of *community*, what does that term mean to you?
2. Describe your experiences of community (beyond your immediate family) in your life right now. Do not limit yourself to the traditional notions of community, but include all interactions with others in which you feel a sense of community.

3. Does the amount of community experience in your life feel too little, too much, or just the right amount?
4. Describe the satisfactions and/or frustrations you experience in your community activities.
5. If you are involved in community activities that are not very satisfying, would you consider letting go of these activities? What can you do to accomplish that goal?
6. What, if any, community activities would you add to your life if you didn't have to work for a living? Can you incorporate some of these activities now and still maintain a reasonable amount of balance? How would you accomplish that goal?

We are not human beings learning to be spiritual; we are spiritual beings learning to be human.

Jacquelyn Small

LOOKING AT THE BIGGER PICTURE . . .

7. How would you describe the community you live in? Is there a lot of interaction and sharing, or do people pretty much keep to themselves? What do you think your community most needs to be stronger?
8. What factors in your culture influence people to have more or less community in their lives?
9. On a societal level, what can be done to increase community sharing without burdening individuals and families?
10. What benefits to society as a whole would flow from greater community sharing?

LIFEWORK ASSIGNMENTS

1. If you feel you don't have enough community in your life, determine what you can do to change this. Then take action, small steps at first, to integrate greater community into your life. This may require letting go of other activities, such as excessive work hours.
2. If you feel burdened by too many community activities, decide which activities have the least value to you and take steps to phase them out of your life. Again, gradual steps in small increments are easiest on all involved.

ANNUAL CHECK-UP

1. Review and respond to questions # 1 through 6 in the lesson assignments above and reflect on how much your life has changed in the last year in terms of community.
2. What are your interests and goals for the coming year in terms of community? Review the lifework assignments above to see if you want to do further work on these tasks.

RECOMMENDED RESOURCES

Books

Cohousing: A Contemporary Approach to Housing Ourselves by Kathryn McCamant and Charles R. Durrett (Berkeley: Ten Speed Press, 2nd edition, 1993). Provides overview of how cohousing communities work, including illustrations of the layout of cohousing communities. Discusses existing cohousing communities in Europe.

Plain & Simple: A Woman's Journey to the Amish by Sue Bender (New York: Harper SF, Reprint 1991). Memoir of author's experiences living in an Amish community. The author reveals the highly interdependent nature of Amish culture, which focuses on mutual support within the community.

Miscellaneous

The Cohousing Network [www.cohousing.org] is an organization whose purpose is to encourage cohousing and support existing and prospective cohousing communities. It offers a database of cohousing communities, a journal, and related resources.

Conversation Cafés [www.conversationcafe.org] is a form of community interaction where people gather in cafés or other public places for 90-minute hosted discussions on important political, social, and cultural issues. Started in 2001 by Vicki Robin, conversation cafés are forming all over the United States and in some other countries.

Intentional Communities [www.ic.org] provides information and resources for the growing communities movement, including ecovillages, cohousing, residential land trusts, communes, student co-ops, urban housing cooperatives and other related projects.

Ithaca Hours [www.ithacahours.org] provides information on the local currency system serving Tompkins County, New York, and a starter kit for setting up a local currency system.

Sustainable Communities Network [www.sustainable.org] is a networking organization whose mission is to support the development of healthy, livable, sustainable communities. Its web site features educational information, news, and related resources in the areas of creating community, smart growth, sustainable economies, protecting natural resources, living sustainably, and governing sustainability.

Time Dollar Institute [www.timedollar.org] is an organization whose purpose is to promote a new medium of exchange called *time dollars*, whereby people convert their personal time into purchasing power by helping others. An hour helping another earns One Time Dollar. The purpose of the *time dollar* program is to rebuild family, neighborhood, and community.

The *Tomales Bay Institute* [www.earthisland.org/tbi], a project of the Earth Island Institute, is a small group of *outside the box* thinkers who are committed to renewing the *commons*, which, as a concept, is broad enough to include everything we inherit as a community—the air we breathe, the words we speak, the traditions that are a part of our culture—as distinguished from what we inherit as individuals.

YES! A Journal of Positive Futures [www.futurenet.org] is a quarterly journal published by *The Positive Futures Network*, an independent, nonprofit organization dedicated to supporting people's active engagement in creating a just, sustainable, and compassionate world. The journal focuses on community building and healing, sustainability, and social justice.

NOTE: *Additions and updates to these resources can be found on The Simplicity Resource Guide at www.gallagherpress.com/pierce.*

LESSON 12

CARING FOR OUR HOME, THE EARTH

SIMPLICITY AND THE EARTH

When I first learned of the voluntary simplicity movement, I devoured every book I could find on the subject—some 50 books over a four-month period. The authors of many of these books discussed the interconnection between simplicity and caring for the earth. At first, I was puzzled. While I was concerned about the environment and had always felt an intense love for nature, I didn't see how simplicity ideals were necessarily related to the natural environment. It seemed to me that a person could be interested in voluntary simplicity for a variety of personal reasons—reduced stress, greater personal freedom, better control of finances—without giving a hoot about the earth.

However, I soon came to learn, through my personal experiences with living more simply and by studying the lives of others, that there is indeed a strong interdependence between living simply and caring for the earth.

It is true that many people are attracted to simplicity because of personal stresses in their lives—too much work and debt, too little time and pleasure. Their initial forays into simplicity are focused on *self-directed* values that enhance the quality of their lives. But once they make progress in those areas, something else happens. They develop an interest in *other-directed* values—interest in community (however small a radius), concern for the earth, and social injustice.

This personal transformation appears to happen naturally and effortlessly. When we slow down the pace of our lives and remove unneeded and unwanted possessions, we free up mental and physical energy. What becomes of this new source of vitality?

I believe that we humans are intrinsically spiritual and compassionate beings. But sometimes it takes a personal tragedy or community crisis to remind us of our compassionate nature. People generally respond with love and caring when others are in desperate need. In these situations, we understand at a deep emotional level how truly connected we are to each other.

Living more simply creates a mental, emotional, and spiritual space that allows our true compassionate nature to come to the surface on an ongoing basis, rather than just at times of crisis. And our compassion is not limited to other people; it extends to the earth herself—to the plants, animals, and ecosystems that exist on our planet.

As discussed in Lesson 8, when we simplify our lives, we become more aware and appreciative of the earth's natural splendors. We develop an innate sense that these life forms are alive, just as we are, and that we are a part of all nature—the trees, animals, and plants. We no longer see ourselves apart from and superior to the natural environment. We are simply one species—while blessed with a superior intelligence—that is intricately bound with all other life forms, from the tiniest protozoa to the cosmos itself. We learn that we need those other life forms much more than they need us.

Unless the gentle inherit the earth, there will be no earth.

May Sarton

This awareness of our mutual dependence leads us to develop real concern, awe, and respect for the earth. We come to understand that our survival (and the survival of those who will live after us) depends on our being good stewards of the environment. We want our great grandchildren to enjoy nutritious food, clean water, and the pleasure of walking along a beach at sunset. Caring for the earth is as much of an expression of our compassionate nature as caring for other people.

HOW BAD IS IT?

As our caring for the earth develops, it's natural to want to understand its condition, to comprehend the many, and sometimes controversial, reports about the state of the earth today. How dire are the predictions of global climate change? Will we run out of fossil fuels? What about diminishing sources of fresh water and agricultural land? Will we have enough resources to feed ourselves in 20 years, in 50 years? Will technological solutions be sufficient to avert future catastrophic disasters? What are the best methods to prevent further deterioration of the earth's resources? One could spend an entire lifetime studying these weighty questions.

While a full discussion of these questions is beyond the scope of this book, the Recommended Resources at the end of this lesson will give you rich opportunities for further study. If you were to read only one book on the state of the earth, I would recommend *Eco-Economy* by Lester R. Brown, President of the Earth Policy Institute and founder of the Worldwatch Institute, publisher of the *State of the World* reports. Published in 2001, this book offers a timely and comprehensive review of the major earth systems at risk and what we can do to avoid the collapse of systems that sustain all life.

While there is some controversy on the best methods to heal the earth, there is a general consensus that life on our planet, at least as we know it today, will not survive to the end of the 21st century if we continue to consume and degrade natural resources at our current rates. Leaders in science, business, and government around the globe acknowledge this sobering fact. In 1992, over 1,500 scientists issued the highly acclaimed *World Scientists' Warning to Humanity* in an attempt to galvanize people throughout the world to take heed—we need to change the way we live, and we need to do it quickly. The scientists' message is clear: "A great change in our stewardship of the earth and the life on it is required if vast human misery is to be avoided and our global home on this planet is not to be irretrievably mutilated."

> *In terms of the biology of the planet*, development *is a euphemism for* destruction.
>
> Helen Caldicott

HOW THE EARTH IS DOING—A PROGRESS REPORT

- Approximately 36 percent of the world's cropland has suffered a loss of productivity due to soil erosion.[1] Today, 420 million people live in countries with insufficient cropland to grow all their own food. By 2025, that number could exceed one billion people.[2]
- Overpumping of water aquifers worldwide approximates 160 billion tons.[3] Over 500 million people live in regions prone to chronic drought. By 2025, that number is likely to expand to 2.4 to 3.4 billion people.[4]
- Annual carbon emissions from fossil fuel combustion reached a record 6.55 billion tons in 2001, the highest level in at least 420,000 years. It is generally agreed that carbon emissions lead to rapid climate change.[5]
- In the last 100 years, forest lands have shrunk from 5 billion hectares (approximately 12.5 billion acres) to 2.9 billion hectares (approximately 7.25 billion acres).[6] Primary tropical forests are disappearing at a rate exceeding 140,000 square kilometers per year.[7]
- Wetlands have been reduced by 50 percent during the last century and 27 percent of the world's coral reefs were severely damaged by 2000.[8]
- Two-thirds of the world's ocean fisheries are being fished at or beyond their sustainable yields.[9]

Whatever we do to any other thing in the great web of life, we do to ourselves, for we are one.

Brooke Medicine Eagle

Each year, we add 77 million people to the planet, the equivalent of 10 New York cities.[10] Some people blame the developing countries with their higher birth rates for the environmental jam our global society is in. But let's examine this more carefully. As of 1998, the top 20 percent of countries (based on income) consumed 58 percent of the world's energy, 65 percent of electricity, 87 percent of automobiles, 74 percent of telephones, 46 percent of meat, and 84 percent of paper.[11] With only five percent of the world's population, the United States alone is responsible for 25 percent of all greenhouse-gas emissions.[12] If the entire world lived like North Americans (and many people want to), we would need at least three planets to live sustainably.[13]

With such inequitable patterns of per capita consumption, perhaps we should first look to ourselves before pointing the finger at developing countries. As Mahatma Ghandi once said, "The world has enough for everyone's need but not for everyone's greed." This is a good thing to remember when you need to remind yourself why you've chosen simplicity.

The future ecological health of the planet will be determined by the convergence of three factors—world population, consumption levels, and technologies used to moderate consumption and waste generation. We need to work hard on all three fronts simultaneously to minimize the loss of human life and the destruction of the ecological systems that support all life.

MAKING A DIFFERENCE

Unfortunately, no single one of us can save the earth. However, each of us does have an impact on the world through our actions. Collectively, how we choose to live our lives will determine the planet's future. We can influence others by our actions (by modeling earth-friendly behavior) and by our words (by sharing our concerns with others), but in the end, we can only be responsible for ourselves. Simplicity is not about imposing beliefs on others or judging their actions. While we can hope to inspire others to care for the earth, we cannot force them to do so, except, of course, by enacting and enforcing laws that mandate sustainable environmental practices.

We can make an even greater contribution if we work in fields that offer the potential to reverse humanity's current destructive patterns, such as alternative energy resources, earth-friendly housing construction, or hydrogen fuel cell transportation. Educating, writing, or working as an activist in environmental fields can also make a difference.

Most of us, however, are not working directly in any of these fields, so our impact is limited primarily to our personal actions. We may ask, "What can *I* do to make a positive difference?" There are many ways that you, personally, can make a contribution. Some are major lifestyle shifts requiring months or years to accomplish, while others are relatively easy adjustments in your daily routine. Here are some examples of earth-friendly choices made by people who live simply:

'Tis the superfluity of one man which makes the poverty of the other.

Vernon Lee

- The Three R's: Reduce, Reuse, and Recycle. This involves *reducing* your level of material consumption, *reusing* what you already have or buying used goods, and *recycling* whatever cannot be reused.
- Live in smaller homes than the United States average of 2,300 square feet (unless you have a large family), thereby reducing the materials used in the initial construction as well as the energy needs for your home once it's completed.
- Shorten the distance between home and work to minimize utilization of fossil fuels. Yes, this may take a house move or a job change.
- Drive vehicles that get a high number of miles per gallon. An even better choice is to drive a hybrid automobile, which uses a combination of gasoline and electric energy. At the time of this writing, automobiles that use fuel cell hydrogen technology are being tested. This technology will not only make a significant contribution to the earth with its zero carbon emissions, but it has the added advantage of eliminating the noise pollution created by gasoline powered vehicles.
- Drive fewer automobile miles, relying instead on public transportation, carpooling, bicycling, and walking for some of your transportation needs.
- Grow and/or eat organic foods. This reduces the amount of harmful pesticides that pollute our air, rivers, and oceans,

threatening the health of humans and the sustainability of fisheries.

- Reduce the amount of meat in your diet. It takes 17 pounds of grain to produce one pound of edible meat.[14] One thousand tons of water are needed to produce one ton of grain.[15] As noted above, our world faces scarcities in both water and in arable land required to grown grain.
- Reduce your use of paper and Styrofoam materials by carrying in your car (or bicycle basket) a coffee cup, a plastic glass, a few refrigerator dishes, and a cloth napkin. When you stop at a café for a drink or a bite to eat, you won't need to use paper or Styrofoam cups, dishware or napkins. You can bring home the leftovers in your own refrigerator dish. This may feel and look weird at first, but if we all did this, we wouldn't give it a second thought.

There is no woe the forest cannot heal, nor any grief.

Mary Carolyn Davies

- Use cloth napkins at home. Use rags and sponges for cleaning up rather than paper towels.
- Use reusable canvas bags to bring home grocery and other shopping items.
- Purchase consumer goods that are manufactured with sustainable practices. You can use the Internet to research which companies and products are manufactured with concern for sustainability. One excellent resource for this purpose is Co-op America (www.coopamerica.org), which publishes an annual directory of products and services called *National Green Pages*.
- Consider joining forces with neighbors and others in your community to implement sustainable living practices. One way of doing this is to establish a Household Ecoteam Program in your neighborhood. This involves five or six households working together, meeting regularly over a period of four months, to support one another in reducing their environmental impacts in the areas of garbage, water, energy, transportation, and consumption. (See the Recommended Resources at the end of this lesson for further information.)

BALANCING ECOLOGICAL PRACTICES WITH THE GOOD LIFE

It's natural to feel overwhelmed, depressed or guilty once we become aware of the serious environmental issues our world faces today. In North America, most of us live in a land of plenty, and it's no small task to abstain from the vast abundance at our fingertips. Many people struggle with the challenge of how to live comfortably without using excessive natural resources.

Feeling guilty or depressed about the environment serves little purpose. As one author, Audre Lorde, puts it: "I have no creative use for guilt, yours or my own. Guilt is only another way of avoiding informed action, of buying time out of the pressing need to make clear choices. . ." The best cure for depression and guilt is positive action, working toward solutions in exactly those areas that trouble you. Without hope, we have no chance of turning the tide of environmental damage.

Deferring gratification is a good definition of being civilized.

Bernice Fitz-Gibbon

Throughout this course, we have reminded ourselves repeatedly that simplicity is not about deprivation. How does this principle fit with our desire for reducing our impact on the earth? When people simplify their lives, they seem to naturally evolve to a point where their personal desires are consistent with sustainable living practices.

Many have found that they can implement earth-friendly practices without diminishing the quality of their lives. It requires a process of experimentation. You may try one thing and find it too restrictive or you may be surprised at how easy it is to make a change. For example, some people turn the Three R's (reduce, reuse, recycle) into a fun game. They derive pleasure from finding great deals at garage sales, repairing something they might otherwise toss into the landfill, or seeing what they can do without. Last year, I tried to go the entire year without buying any clothes, new or used. I didn't make it—a sweater in Ireland and new hiking boots were irresistible—but it was fun to try.

A friend of mine has always been able to find mechanics who take great pride in rebuilding certain cars. These mechanics have rebuilt my friend's 20-year old Volvo's, making them safe and dependable for another 100,000 to 150,000 miles. Rebuilding these cars saves natural resources and reduces waste as well as pollution.

Others find these types of activities onerous or burdensome, but may take other steps to reduce their consumption on the earth, perhaps in their choices of housing or by using public transportation. Most people do not make wholesale changes but gradually incorporate more earth-friendly practices over time.

It's important to accept where you are on the consumption ladder and start from there. If you live a highly consumptive lifestyle, don't try to change it all at once. If you can reduce your impact on the earth gradually over time, you are not likely to feel deprived. Sometimes all it takes is education and awareness to motivate us to let go of unfavorable practices. Listen to your heart. Your compassionate nature will lead you to do what you can.

I change myself,
I change the world.

Gloria Anzaldúa

In many instances we would be as happy or happier with less materialism in our lives. We know this intuitively. The key is to pay attention to what provides the real quality in your life. It's all about *mindful living*, which is as good a two-word description of simplicity as any.

HOW SOCIAL AND PUBLIC POLICIES CAN HELP

As lives of simplicity mature, one becomes increasingly concerned and aware of how much we must do to address the environmental problems facing us all. We often find ourselves looking beyond our own actions to what needs to be done on a societal level to move toward a healthier planet.

In previous lessons, we considered the use of earth taxes and credits to encourage practices that preserve natural resources, such as taxes on excessively large homes (see Lesson 4), luxury items (see Lesson 2), and gasoline usage (see Lesson 7). The point is not to deprive people of the freedom to consume as they choose, but rather to ask them to pay for the true cost of their consumption choices. There is nothing quite like a financial incentive to give us motivation, individually and collectively, to find other, less damaging ways to live.

European countries have taken the lead in implementing green taxes. Finland, Sweden, Denmark, and the Netherlands have imposed various taxes on carbon outputs, resulting in reduced usage. In some instances, these taxes have facilitated a corresponding reduction of income taxes.[16] In addition to tax incentives, the governments of industrialized countries, as well as private investors, would be wise to fund the development of alternative energy sources such as wind and solar. This is less an altruistic measure than an investment in future economic health and quality of life.

In Lesson 2, I mentioned Ireland's tax on the distribution of plastic bags by retailers, resulting in a 90 percent decline of plastic bag usage. This simple, effective tax is a wonderful example of creating a financial incentive to take action in ways that are not burdensome. Similarly, we could impose taxes on the use of Styrofoam cups and dishware, giving people the incentive to bring their own cups to the local coffee house.

Socialism collapsed because it did not allow prices to tell the economic truth. Capitalism may collapse because it does not allow prices to tell the ecological truth.

Øystein Dahle

Another favorable policy would be to expand requirements for manufacturers to close the material loop—to assume full responsibility for whatever they produce, including recycling the waste at the end of their products' useful life.

When the subject of reducing consumption is discussed, some people express concern about the economy—how many jobs would be lost if we stop buying and consuming so much? This is short-sighted thinking in a number of ways. First, if we were to impose consumption taxes, we could phase them in gradually (but not too long because we don't have that long) to give people an adjustment period. Second, while we may eliminate certain jobs in manufacturing and retailing, building an eco-economy, as explained by Lester R. Brown in his book, *Eco-Economy*, would create many new jobs and professions. For example, engineers could be retrained to design and build wind generators. The construction and mechanic trades would be needed to install and maintain such alternative energy sources. Similarly, new jobs would be created in the areas of hydrogen generation, fuel cell manufacturing and solar cell manufacturing.

And finally, there is an equally important question to consider: what will happen to our economy if we continue at our present rate of consumption and waste generation? For example, the rise in carbon dioxide is widely believed to cause the earth's temperature to rise, which in turn leads to stronger storm systems and natural disasters. The economic losses from storm disturbances are massive. Soaring insurance costs, widespread damage to property and community infrastructure, and damage to soil and other natural resources are just a few examples.[17] It is economic suicide to continue on our current path of consumption.

Social and public policies that encourage the formation of livable towns and cities (see Lesson 4 for a discussion of this trend) can make a significant contribution to preserving the earth's resources. If we reduce the distances we need to travel for work and other daily needs, we will reduce automobile-driven miles substantially. If we shop locally, we further reduce the transportation burden on the earth.

Greed stains our culture, soaks our sensibilities, and has replaced grace as a sign of our intimacy with the divine.

Jennifer Stone

Undoubtedly, there are other ways social and public policies can encourage living more lightly on the earth. In the lesson assignments below, you will have an opportunity to develop your own ideas.

CONCLUSION

In contemplating our relationship to the earth, we might learn from the Hippocratic Oath taken by physicians to *first, do no harm*. It is fortunate that living more simply both enhances our personal quality of life and preserves the earth's resources. It's a win-win situation. To the extent that we educate ourselves on the true state of the world today, we are more likely to be motivated to reduce our impact on the earth.

LESSON ASSIGNMENTS

FROM YOUR PERSONAL VIEWPOINT . . .

1. When and how did you first develop an interest in caring for the earth? Has your interest in simplicity changed your attitudes about caring for the earth?
2. What earth-friendly practices do your currently engage in? Describe any particular burdens or pleasures associated with these activities.
3. Take a test to measure your *ecological footprint*. This mea-

Ponder it for a few days.

Then begin to apply yourself to the Lesson Assignments.

Make some notes to share at the meeting.

Each meeting will begin with a 2-3 minute “check in” with each person.

Moderator will introduce the session topic.

Break in to groups of 3 to discuss our experiences with the lesson assignments for approx 30 minutes.

Come back together to brainstorm Looking at the Bigger Picture.

Close meeting.

Simplicity Circle Information

At our first meeting we will create a contact list to share with all members.

Each meeting needs a moderator. I will get us started, and after a few sessions we'll solicit volunteers.

This process does not lend itself well to adding new members after we get started. New members will only be added if EVERYONE in the group agrees. You'll see how easy it is to start a circle, if you know people who would like to join, they can start another one.

Meeting dates: March 16, 30

April 20

May 4, 18

June 1, 15, 29

July 13, 27

August 10, 24

Format for each meeting:

Read the lesson at least a week before each meeting

surement translates your natural resource utilization and waste generation into a productive land area that is needed to sustain your living practices. There are several tests available on the Internet (for example, see www.lead.org/leadnet/footprint or www.earthday.net/footprint). You can also search for others by typing "ecological footprint" in the search engine of your choice.

4. What earth-friendly practices would you like to adopt in the future? Does guilt play a role in your interests? Do you anticipate feeling deprived if you adopt these practices? What do you need to do in your life to accomplish these goals?

There's a thread that binds all of us together, pull one end of the thread, the strain is felt all down the line.

Rosamond Marshall

LOOKING AT THE BIGGER PICTURE . . .

5. How much interest in environmental issues is there in your community? Do you feel accepted by or isolated from the community when you engage in earth-friendly practices?
6. What social or public policies do you think would motivate people to live more sustainable lifestyles? How might they be implemented?

LIFEWORK ASSIGNMENTS

1. Design a plan for what you want to do within the coming year to reduce your impact on the earth. Be realistic. If you intend to make a big change, such as reducing the number of cars in your family by one, write down what interim steps are needed, such as organizing a ride share to work, to accomplish your goal. Monitor your progress periodically, perhaps quarterly.
2. Consider participating in a community group or process that is committed to preserving the earth's resources. For example, you may want to participate in a Household Ecoteam Program (see the Recommended Resources below). Or perhaps you may want to volunteer for programs that directly care for the earth, for example, litter removal or habitat restoration programs.

ANNUAL CHECK-UP

1. Remeasure your ecological footprint (see # 3 under the lesson assignments above). How does it compare to your footprint one year ago?
2. Review what steps you have taken during the last year to reduce your impact on the earth.
3. Design a plan for what environmental choices you want to make during the coming year.

If we all tried to make other people's paths easy, our own feet would have a smooth even place to walk on.

Myrtle Reed

RECOMMENDED RESOURCES

Books

Eco-Economy: Building an Economy for the Earth by Lester R. Brown (New York: W.W. Norton, 2001). Founding Director of the Earth Policy Institute explores how our current economic model negatively impacts natural resources. Provides comprehensive solutions towards an eco-economy, such as tax shifts to encourage sustainable business practices.

Beyond the Limits: Confronting Global Collapse, Envisioning A Sustainable Future by Donella H. Meadows, Dennis L. Meadows, and Jøgern Randers (Post Mills, VT: Chelsea Green Publishing, Reprint 1993). Scholarly sequel to the international bestseller, *Limits to Growth*, published in 1972. Uses a systems analysis approach to review sustainability issues of population and capital growth, planetary sources for materials and energy, and the planet's ability to recycle or absorb the pollutants we create.

Confronting Consumption by Thomas Princen, Michael Maniates, and Ken Conca (eds.) (Cambridge, MA: MIT Press, 2002). Scholars from the University of Michigan, Allegheny College, and University of Maryland recommend confronting consumption as a driving focus of the environmental movement, with a strong voluntary simplicity component.

EarthScore: Your Personal Environmental Audit & Guide by Donald W. Lotter (Lafayette, Ca: Morning Sun Press, 1993). Detailed workbook that helps you measure your lifestyle practices in the areas of household energy, water, transportation, consumerism, toxins, wastes, recycling and related topics. Recommendations and resources are included.

Living More with Less by Doris Janzen Longacre (Scottdale, PA: Herald Press, 1980). Discusses the finite nature of the earth's resources and the need for the *haves* of this world to reduce their consumption of resources so that the *have-nots* have a shot at obtaining basic necessities of life.

Natural Capitalism: Creating the Next Industrial Revolution by Paul Hawken, Amory Lovins, and L. Hunter Lovins (New York: Back Bay Books, 2000). Presents a vision for the next industrial revolution that can enhance productivity and efficiency, create new jobs, and preserve the earth's resources. The term *natural capitalism* is based on the principle that business can be good for the environment.

Our Ecological Footprint: Reducing Human Impact on the Earth by Mathis Wackernagel and William E. Rees (Gabriola Island, B.C.: New Society Publishers, 1995). Presents concept of ecological footprint—the amount of productive land area (based on resource consumption and waste assimilation requirements) needed to sustain the lifestyle of an individual or a defined population—as a tool for measuring humanity's impact on the earth. Suggests alternative ways of living to reduce footprint.

Promise Ahead: A Vision of Hope and Action for Humanity's Future by Duane Elgin (New York: Quill, 2001). Evolutionary activist examines adversity trends (such as population growth and depletion of natural resources) and opportunity trends (such as simple living and use of the Internet as a tool for social change) facing the global world today. Discusses the power and significance of the evolutionary turning point at which we find ourselves.

Shoveling Fuel for a Runaway Train: Errant Economists, Shameful Spenders, and a Plan to Stop Them All by Brian Czech (Berkeley: University of California Press, 2000). Challenges North America's love affair with economic growth. Offers a thorough yet accessible review of economic theory, including the traditional theory of neoclassical economics and the new paradigm of ecological economics. Proposes a *steady state* economy as an alternative to unlimited growth.

Small is Beautiful: Economics as if People Mattered: 25 Years Later…With Commentaries by E.F. Schumacher (Point Roberts, WA: Hartley & Marks, 2nd edition, 1999, first published in 1973). Classic text written by a visionary British economist. The author exposes the damaging and short-sighted aspects of Western economies, specifically the desire for ever increasing growth without concern for non-renewable sources of energy. Includes commentary and practical suggestions for solving world-wide problems of inequality of wealth and poverty in developing countries.

Stepping Lightly: Simplicity for People and the Planet by Mark A. Burch (Gabriola Island, B.C.: New Society Publishers, 2000). Goes beyond the benefits of voluntary simplicity for individuals to reveal how its practice can serve as a thoughtful approach to solving modern social and environmental problems.

The Unsettling of America: Culture & Agriculture by Wendell Berry (San Francisco: Sierra Club, 3rd edition, 1996). Poet/farmer writes eloquently about consequences of being divorced from the land. Explores damaging impact of modern American agriculture on our culture, health, economy, relationships, and spiritual lives.

MISCELLANEOUS

Co-op America [www.coopamerica.org] is a membership-based, nonprofit organization whose mission is to further a socially just and environmentally sustainable society. It offers educational programs, a national green pages of compatible business listings, a quarterly journal, and more.

Earth Day Network [www.earthday.net] is an alliance of 5,000 groups in 184 countries working to promote a healthy environment and a peaceful, just, sustainable world. It organizes and coordinates an international Earth Day event in April of each year. It also sponsors related campaigns and educational programs throughout the year.

Earthsave [www.earthsave.org], founded by John Robbins, author of *Diet for a New America* and *The Food Revolution*, promotes a shift to a healthy, plant-based diet. It offers educational materials and support through membership in local chapters.

EcoIQ Magazine [www.ecoiq.com/magazine] is an online quarterly journal dedicated to building sustainable communities. Its focus is on decisions that are both economically *and* ecologically intelligent. Its web site is comprehensive, offering current news briefs, feature articles, and other resources.

Household Ecoteam Program [www.globalactionplan.org] is offered by *The Empowerment Institute* (formally Global Action Plan), whose mission is to empower the human dimension of community and environmental change. The Household Ecoteam

Program provides materials and support for small groups of neighbors to work together to reduce their environmental impact in the areas of garbage, water, electricity, transportation, and consumption.

The Institute for Deep Ecology [www.deep-ecology.org] promotes ecological values and actions by providing opportunities for inquiry and practice through workshops, publications, and support networks.

Northwest Earth Institute [www.nwei.org] is a Portland-based organization that offers courses on voluntary simplicity, deep ecology, and sustainable living. The courses consist of weekly discussion groups based on readings from a course book that includes a diverse collection of essays, articles, and book excerpts.

Rocky Mountain Institute [www.rmi.org] is a research and consulting nonprofit organization that works with businesses, governments, communities, and individuals to advance resource efficiency market-based solutions. The book, *Natural Capitalism*, was authored by its founders and Paul Hawken.

Worldwatch Institute [www.worldwatch.org], founded by Lester Brown in 1974, is a leader in interdisciplinary research with a global focus in the areas of environmental sustainability and social justice. It publishes the well-known annual *State of the World* reports, *Vital Signs*, and the *Worldwatch Paper* series.

NOTE: *Additions and updates to these resources can be found on The Simplicity Resource Guide at www.gallagherpress.com/pierce.*

EPILOGUE

Where Do We Go From Here?

Now that we have completed our final lesson, you may be tempted to ask (much as the little kid in the backseat), "Are we there yet?" Simplifying your life is not accomplished in a few weeks, or even a few months. Many people need an initial period of three to five years to make basic changes toward a life of simplicity. And you never really get there. Simplicity is not a destination but a life-long process, a way of looking at life, a form of mindful living that will take on different shapes as you go through life. Recognize that what may be a life of simplicity for you now might look radically different in 10 years. Refinements and adjustments are ongoing.

So, where do we go from here? Reading can be a great source of inspiration and learning. Look over the Recommended Resources in each lesson to see what appeals to you. As you expand your knowledge, you will discover new meaning and opportunities to live more simply.

Some simplicity study groups decide to continue meeting after the course is over. They might meet once a month to share what is going on in each of their lives—their progress and concerns as it relates to simplicity. Some groups will select a different book as a focus for discussion for each session.

This course, as well as any supplemental reading you do, is a first step. But reading and talking are not enough. You need to experiment with applying the principles of simplicity to all aspects of your life. Focus on taking small, gradual steps. Use the *lifework assignments* and the *annual check-up* tasks in each lesson to practice the art of simplicity and monitor your progress. And don't forget—what simplicity is for one person may be deprivation for another. A good simplicity mantra to keep in mind is *No Shame, No Blame* (popularized by the bestselling book, *Your Money or Your Life* by Joe Dominguez and Vicki Robin).

It takes courage and healthy self-esteem to live simply—to define yourself *not* by conventional values, not by what corporate advertisers would have you believe you need to be happy, but by the work, relationships, and activities that give you genuine meaning and purpose in your life. You have already taken great strides on this path of courage. You should pat yourself on the back for doing the work this course asked of you. It is substantial.

As people who are drawn to the concepts of simplicity, what should our attitudes be about others who work and spend excessively or consume in ways that harm the earth? In my view, there is no place for a holier-than-thou attitude with simplicity. As we've seen, simplicity is, in its most essential form, an inside job. It must come from within. Yes, we can be inspired and educated by the actions and writings of others, but living simply has no meaning unless it is embraced voluntarily and joyfully.

Why walk when you can fly?

Mary Chapin Carpenter

I wish you the very best on your journey. If you would like to share your story, I would love to hear it. You can email me at pierce@gallagherpress.com. I may not be able to respond to you right away, but rest assured that I will read and enjoy your messages. For now, I bid goodbye to you with one of my favorite Irish blessings:

These things, I warmly wish for you—
Someone to love,
Some work to do,
A bit of o' sun
A bit o' cheer
And a guardian angel
Always near.

APPENDIX A

THE SIMPLICITY STUDY GROUP

NUTS & BOLTS

There are a number of logistical factors to study groups that contribute to a positive group experience. The following guidelines are based on the experiences of many simplicity study groups. However, feel free to vary these procedures if you feel your situation warrants it.

SIZE OF GROUP

A group of 10 to 12 members is an ideal size. Often, there are one or two people who can't attend a specific meeting, leaving 8 to 10 people for any one session. This size is optimal for discussion and participation by all members.

It may take a few sessions to establish who wants to be in the group. Some may decide after one or two sessions that it is not for them. Others will hear about the group and want to join. Adding new members after the first two or three sessions should be done only if all members agree. A certain level of trust and confidence develops in the group, and it can be disruptive to add new members midway through.

LENGTH OF COURSE

This guide is designed for 12 sessions, one for each lesson in this book, but some groups continue for years. After completing an initial study course, the group may meet periodically, often once a month, to discuss simplicity-related books and their ongoing progress with living simply. A group might also work together on simplicity-related social or public policy changes. The Recommended Resources at the end of each lesson offer many choices for subsequent study and discussion.

It is wise for the group to commit to a minimum of 8 to 12 sessions at the beginning of the course. If you are considering joining a group and know in advance that you will need to miss more than two or three sessions, it's best to pass on this group and wait until your schedule frees up. The group loses some of its strength if some members are inactive.

WHEN AND WHERE TO MEET

I recommend either weekly or biweekly meetings. If you meet less frequently, you are likely to lose continuity and community in the group process. Meeting every other week has the advantage of giving people plenty of time to reflect on the lessons and do the exercises.

The sessions are designed to last 90 minutes to two hours. It's important to start and stop on time so members can honor other priorities in their lives. The group should select a time and day that works best for everyone.

In some groups, a member who enjoys hosting will offer his or her home as a gathering place for the meetings. In other groups, members will rotate hosting duties. Another possibility is a public café or meeting place, provided it offers a fair amount of quiet and privacy. Community rooms in churches or libraries are sometimes available.

Whether to have refreshments or not is a group decision. If you decide to have refreshments, you may want to take turns providing them. Depending on the time of day, you may want to keep it simple with tea, coffee, or cold drinks. You may be tempted to serve wine or beer at an early evening meeting, but resist. It's too easy for the group to slip into an unfocused social gathering. Such social gatherings are wonderful, but they won't serve the learning purpose of your study group meeting. That's not to say that your study group meeting can't be filled with humor and fun, but make it sober fun. You can always have your study group meeting first, followed by a glass of wine and potluck goodies.

THE MODERATOR

A moderator should be designated for each session. It's important to remember that the moderator is not a teacher or a leader but rather a coordinator. The role of the moderator is to start the session on time, direct the members to split into smaller groups or gather as one large group (see Appendix B for instructions), and call an end to the meeting.

It's wise to select moderators from those who enjoy this role. Some people don't enjoy it and are terrible at it. Others have a natural affinity for it. Ask for volunteers. Some groups rotate members as moderators. In other groups, one person volunteers to moderate the entire course to everyone's satisfaction. It is not a difficult job. All you need to do is follow the guidelines in Appendix B.

THE GROUP PROCESS

In a study group, all members have an equal right to express their views. There are certain techniques that facilitate this objective. One is the use of *break-out* groups. For a certain portion of each session, a group of 8 to 12 members will break up into two or three smaller groups of three to five people. This allows each person to have more time to talk about his personal concerns and ideas related to the topic for that lesson. Then the smaller groups reunite into one large group to discuss the lesson topics from a broader point of view.

Another method to encourage full participation by group members is the use of a *talking stick*. This is some small object—anything small enough to hold in one's hand will work—that each person holds while he or she is talking. When one person holds the talking stick, it's a reminder to everyone else that it's the speaker's turn to talk. This helps the speaker feel freer to take the floor, and it makes it easier for others to really listen. Holding an object while talking also helps the speaker remember that he has a limited time to talk. When the speaker is finished, he passes the talking stick to the next person. By going around the circle, each person has a chance to talk without having to push his way into the conversation. It's helpful to use a talking stick in both the large group and small group discussions, so you will need at least two, possibly three, objects. It works well for the host of each meeting to supply the talking sticks if the meetings are held in private homes. Otherwise, the moderator can bring the talking sticks.

A third technique to facilitate full participation is to use a timer, at least initially, to guide members on how much time they take for their turns. For each portion of the session, there are recommended time limits (see Appendix B). Some people have difficulty sensing a three-minute space of time and can easily spend 10 minutes talking without realizing it. Until everyone gets the hang of it, it's useful for the moderator to use some sort of timer—preferably something quiet and unobtrusive like a stopwatch—to track the time each member spends talking. If a member greatly exceeds his allotted time, the moderator can gently remind the person to finish his thought and come to a close.

HOW TO START A SIMPLICITY STUDY GROUP IN YOUR COMMUNITY

Ok, let's say you have picked up this book and are ready to start a simplicity study group. What next? It's easier than you might think. First, select a date and time at least several weeks in the future for an orientation meeting. The orientation meeting should last for approximately one hour. If you are comfortable hosting this meeting at your home, this is generally easier than finding a public place. Next, you will want to let people in your community know of this meeting. You can post fliers on community bulletin boards at coffee houses, grocery stores, libraries, and churches. See Appendix D for a sample flier. You can also submit a notice or press release to your local newspapers to get this event included in their calendar sections. See Appendix C for a sample press release. It's wise to publicize the event a few days to a week before the orientation meeting. Call the newspapers to find out how much time in advance they need the press release before it shows up in the calendar listings.

Make sure that your flier and press release require people to call or email you if they want to attend the orientation meeting. Otherwise, you could end up with many more people than you can accommodate. If more than 12 to 15 people express interest, you will likely need a public place for the orientation meeting. In that event, you might also need to form two groups. If that seems too much to organize, then you can limit attendance at the orientation meeting to no more than 15 people. Perhaps someone else will want to start a second group.

ORIENTATION MEETING

The following is a list of tasks to complete at the orientation meeting:

1. Invite each person to introduce himself and describe briefly (in a few minutes) his interest in simplicity.
2. Introduce this book to the group and read the topics listed in the table of contents. Give the group a brief overview of the study group process, as outlined in this Appendix A.
3. Decide how many sessions (from 8 to 12) the group wants to commit to. If it is fewer than 12 sessions, select which topics to exclude, but be sure to include Lesson 1.
4. Select a regular day and time for meetings. Decide whether to meet weekly or biweekly.
5. Select a place or places to meet. This may require research into available public places if members don't want to host the meetings in their homes. Ask for one or two volunteers to make calls to find out what meeting places are available in your community.
6. Decide as a group what you want to do about refreshments at your meetings. The place or places you decide to meet will obviously influence the choice of refreshments served.
7. Select one or more moderators. Ask for volunteers. If people have a particular interest in one or more topics, they might want to volunteer to moderate that topic's session.
8. At the conclusion of the meeting, circulate a piece of paper for each person to list his name, address, phone number(s), and email address, if any.

As the person getting this group started, you should take notes of the decisions made by the group. After this orientation meeting, type up a list of names and contact information, the dates, times, locations, moderators, and topics for each session. At your first session or before, distribute this master list to all members. You may need to update it from time to time. Email communications are ideal if most members use email.

APPENDIX B

AGENDA FOR SIMPLICITY STUDY GROUP SESSIONS

OPENING

The moderator should ask everyone to be seated for the start of the session. Ideally, the seating would be arranged in a circle so that each person can easily see everyone else.

CHECK-IN

The moderator can then invite each person, using the *talking stick*, to spend a few (two to three) minutes sharing whatever personal simplicity-related thoughts he or she chooses. It's easiest if people simply take turns around the circle. This can relate to lifework assignments from previous lessons, an announcement of progress with simplicity goals (however humble), concern about a simplicity-related challenge in his life, an insight realized since the last session, or any other simplicity-related thought or concern.

TOTAL APPROXIMATE TIME: 30 MINUTES.

TOPIC FOR THIS LESSON

The moderator will then introduce the topic for this session by describing it briefly. At that point, the moderator will break up the group into small groups of three to five people for the small group discussion.

TOTAL APPROXIMATE TIME: 5 MINUTES.

SMALL GROUP DISCUSSION

Using a talking stick, each person is encouraged to share his or her reflections on some or all the questions raised in the *From Your Personal Viewpoint* section of the lesson assignments for the lesson being discussed. Others in the group should feel free to offer any reactions or constructive suggestions, always keeping in mind that we are here to help each other learn, and a supportive environment contributes to that process. Each person should feel free to take up to 10 minutes for his or her turn.

TOTAL APPROXIMATE TIME: 40–50 MINUTES.

Large Group Discussion

After gathering everyone into one large group, the moderator can read the questions posed in the *Looking at the Bigger Picture* section of the lesson assignments. All members are encouraged to participate in a general brainstorming discussion of these issues. If you find that people are interrupting each other or that some people are left out of the discussion, the moderator can resume the use of the talking stick.

Total approximate time: 20 minutes.

Lifework Assignments

To conclude the meeting, the moderator will invite each person to share which, if any, of the lifework assignments for that lesson he or she chooses to undertake.

Total approximate time: 15 minutes.

Conclusion

The moderator should confirm the date and location of the next meeting and then bring the session to a close.

APPENDIX C

SAMPLE PRESS RELEASE

NOTE: the address of the orientation meeting is purposely not included in the press release. You want to know how many people plan to attend, so it's best to make them call to RSVP and you can then give them the location of the meeting.

[date] — **For Immediate Release**

To: [name of newspaper and the name of the calendar editor, if you know it]

Contact: [your name, address, phone, and email address]

Simplicity Study Discussion Group Starting Soon

A simplicity study discussion group based on the book, *Simplicity Lessons: A 12-Step Guide to Living Simply*, will start soon. The group will meet biweekly for 12 sessions on dates and at times determined by the participants. Topics include material consumption, money, work, housing, time, transportation, travel, inner simplicity, health, relationships, community, and the environment. There is no charge for this course.

An orientation meeting will be held on [date], starting at [start time] for about one hour. Contact [your name] at [your phone number] or [your email address] for further information or to make a reservation for the orientation meeting, at which time you will be given the location for the meeting and other information.

APPENDIX D

SAMPLE FLIER TO START A SIMPLICITY STUDY GROUP

Simplicity Study Discussion Group Starting Soon!

Want to learn about living more simply?

Join a group of 8 to 10 people for a simplicity study discussion group that will meet biweekly for 12 sessions. The date and time of the meetings will be determined by the participants.

Topics include material consumption, money, work, housing, time, transportation, travel, inner simplicity, health, relationships, community, and the environment.

We will use the book, *Simplicity Lessons: A 12-Step Guide to Living Simply* by Linda Breen Pierce, as a guide for this course.

This program is free!!!!

Orientation meeting:
Saturday, [date], [start time] to [end time]

To RSVP and get directions for the orientation meeting, or for further information, contact [your name] at [your phone number] or [your email address].

HOURLY COMPENSATION WORKSHEET

A. TIME CALCULATION: Enter the number of hours spent on each task. All figures should be WEEKLY estimates.

Type of Work	Official Hours	Overtime	Commute Time	Grooming for Work	Time spent "decompressing" from work	Work-related errands	Other	Total Adjusted Hours

B. COST OF WORKING: All figures should be weekly estimates.

Type of Work	Income Taxes	Wardrobe (for work)	Grooming (for work)	Excess Cost for Lunches	Excess Cost for Dinners	Commute Costs	Child Care	House cleaning	Yard Work	Other	Total Costs

C. TRUE HOURLY COMPENSATION (this section to be filled out for paid work only):

First, enter your weekly compensation: $ ____________ **

Then, subtract your Total Work Costs: $ ____________

And you get: $ ____________ (This figure is your Adjusted Weekly Compensation)

Next, divide your Adjusted Weekly Compensation by your Total Adjusted Hours

And you get: $ ____________ (This figure is your True Hourly Compensation)

** Note: include in your weekly compensation the weekly value of any benefits you would otherwise spend money on, for example, health benefits, retirement benefits, fitness programs.

To download a copy of this worksheet, log on to: www.gallagherpress.com/charts.htm

MONEY WORKSHEET

To download a copy of this worksheet, log on to: www.gallagherpress.com/charts.htm

If you already monitor your income and expenses, you should be able to fill out this worksheet fairly easily. However, if this is new to you, consider doing the following exercise. For a one-month period, keep track of all the money that comes into and goes out of your life. Be vigilant but don't worry about keeping track of every last penny. After that one-month period, you will be able to prepare this worksheet with intelligent estimates. You will also need to refer to your checkbook register and/or prior credit card statements for some items, such as insurance, taxes, and other periodic expenses. If you are a member of a household that pools its income and shares its expenses, include totals from the household.

A. Money Coming Into Your Life (Monthly Estimates)

_________ Wages, salary

_________ Self-employment income (net amount after business expenses but before taxes)

_________ Interest and investment income

___725___ Pension and social security income

_________ Alimony and child support payments

_________ ______________________________

_________ ______________________________

_________ ______________________________

_________ ______________________________

_________ ______________________________

_________ ______________________________

___725___ **Total Money Coming Into Your Life**

B. Money Going Out of Your Life (Monthly Estimates)

_________ Income Taxes

_________ Housing Costs (rent or mortgage. If you own your home, monthly prorated amounts of property taxes, maintenance, and insurance)

___125___ Utilities (gas, electric, water, sewer, trash, etc.)

___70___ Housecleaning and yard expenses, if any

___35___ Phone

___61.___ Cable TV, if any

(5) 48 + 36(9) Automobile expenses (lease or loan payments, if any, gas, insurance, maintenance, registration and license, automobile plans)

_________ Other transportation expenses (bus, subway, cost of bicycle if used for transportation, etc.)

50 Food (dining in) and general household supplies

________ Dining out (include snacks, e.g., cappuccinos)

________ Other entertainment (movies, plays, concerts, etc.)

________ Sports and exercise activities (gym fees, athletic events, etc.)

________ Vacations and travel

________ Clothing, accessories, and personal care items

________ Computers and software

________ Other "stuff" (books, furnishings, everything but clothes, computers, and gifts. Or if you have substantial expenses in one area, list as a separate item below)

________ Gifts to others

113 Medical and dental insurance premiums

________ Medical, dental, and prescription expenses not covered by insurance

________ Children (additional expenses such as child care, special activities, education, etc. List as separate items if substantial)

________ ________________________

________ ________________________

________ ________________________

________ ________________________

________ ________________________

________ ________________________

________ ________________________

________ ________________________

________ ________________________

________ ________________________

________ ________________________

________ ________________________

________ **Total Expenses**

C. Summary

735 Total Money Coming In (see A. above)

________ Subtract Total Money Going Out (see B. above)

________ Net Funds Available for Saving

TIME INVENTORY WORKSHEET

To download a copy of this worksheet, log on to: www.gallagherpress.com/charts.htm

Column A: Write down the estimated hours you spend on each activity. The activity categories listed below are merely suggestions. Feel free to delete, add to, or modify these categories to reflect your lifestyle. Some activities may apply to more than one category. For example, a solitary nature walk could be a spiritual practice, a form of exercise, and a form of recreation. Enter the time in only one category, the one you associate it with most. All figures should be weekly estimates, based on your typical week. Be sure that your total weekly hours add up to 168.

Column B: Rate activities for their intrinsic value, with "1" being the highest value. So, for example, while commuting may be necessary for my job, it does not have intrinsic value (I would just as soon not do it), so it clearly would not rate a "1" (high value). If it is a source of stress and fatigue, I might rate it a "3" (low value). If I feel neutral about it, I would rate it a "2" (medium value).

Column C: If you were to design the lifestyle of your choice, list the hours you would spend on each activity. Be sure that your total weekly hours add up to 168.

Activity	A. Actual Hours	B. Rating 1 to 3	C. Ideal Hours
Sleep	H 9		
Bathing, grooming	7		
Meal preparation (shopping, cooking)	(10		
Eating meals			
Physical exercise			
Spiritual - prayer, church services, meditation, journal writing, etc.	4		
Education/personal growth activities - reading, seminars, etc.			
Artistic/Creative Activities - participating in art, music, singing, dancing, etc.			
Personal business (paying bills, tending to insurance, taxes, shopping for necessities, etc.)			
Work (whether paid or volunteer) - actual work hours			
Work - hours spent to support work (commute time, getting ready for work, ironing work clothes, etc.)			
Parenting (this relates primarily to actual parenting chores; see the next item relating to recreational time spent with family)			
Recreational time spent with family and friends			
Entertainment and hobbies (you might want to break this into categories if you spend large amounts of time on a specific hobby or entertainment, such as golf, shopping as a form of entertainment, watching television)			
Time spent "vegging out" (mind-numbing activities that you don't enjoy that much but you are too tired to do anything else)			
Service to family (other than parenting) and friends			
Time spent in community activities beyond friends			
TOTAL HOURS	**168**		**168**

ANALYSIS-BUY OR RENT YOUR RESIDENCE

To download a copy of this worksheet, log on to: www.gallagherpress.com/charts.htm

NOTE: the median time people live in a home in the U.S. is 5.2 years; therefore, this example is based on a 5 year period. Figures are rounded off to the nearest dollar.

Option A: Buy a home for $300,000, live in it for five years, then sell it.

MONTHLY COSTS	ANNUAL COSTS	
$ 218	$ 2,610	Opportunity cost of 20% down payment ($60,000). This figure is based on a 6% return on your down payment money if you rented instead of buying a home, further reduced by the income taxes on the interest at a tax rate of 27.5%.[1]
$ 870	$ 10,444	Mortgage on $240,000 (interest only based on a rate of 6%, principal not included as you will get your principal back when you sell. Amount is further reduced by income tax savings on the interest portion at a tax rate of 27.5%.
$ 284	$ 3,412	Property Taxes (California rates are used in this example; substitute your state's property tax rate here.)
$ 50	$ 600	Property Insurance (covering liability and property damage from casualties such as fire, floods, earthquakes, and hurricanes. Check your local rates).
$ 200	$ 2,400	Maintenance Expenses (including both routine maintenance and capital improvements such as new appliances, roof replacement, heating system, etc. Your estimate may vary depending on condition of home, local costs, and how much you can do yourself.)
$ 1,622	$ 19,466	TOTAL OPERATING EXPENSES FOR PURCHASE OPTION
Further Adjustments		
$ 400	$ 4,800	Expenses of selling the home after five years, including a 6% real estate commission on a selling price of $364,996 (based on a 4% annual appreciation from date of purchase) and miscellaneous closing costs. In this example, closing costs are estimated at $24,000, representing an average annual cost of $4,800 over 5 years.
$ (1,083)	$ (13,000)	Offset for annual appreciation, estimated at approximately 4% per year. The amount of expected appreciation should be taken into account when figuring the costs of home ownership. Call the local association for real estate agents to find out what the appreciation rate has been in your area. Since this is a speculative estimate at best, be conservative.
$ 939	$ 11,266	TOTAL ADJUSTED COSTS OF HOME OWNERSHIP

Option B: Rent a Home Starting at $800 per month for five years

$ 850	$ 10,200	Average annual rental, based on a starting rent of $800 per month, increasing by $25 per month for each of the next five years.
$ 13	$ 150	Renter's insurance covering liability, theft, and personal property damage. Use local rates.
$ 863	$ 10,350	TOTAL ADJUSTED COSTS OF RENTING A HOME

Results: In this example it is more expensive to buy than to rent by an amount of $916 per year or $76.30 per month.

[1] To calculate your oppportunity cost, multiply the amount of your down payment funds by the expected rate of annual return you would receive if you invested your down payment funds elsewhere. Then deduct from that figure the amount of income taxes you would pay on that income based on your tax rate.

TRANSPORTATION INVENTORY WORKSHEET

(Illustrative Example)

TRANSPORTATION	ACTIVITY	TIME SPENT EACH WEEK	MILES TRAVELED
Walking	Walk to and from train station for work	20 min/day x 5 days/week = 1 hour, 40 minutes	5
Train	Commute to work	40 min/day x 5 days/week = 3 hours, 20 minutes	180
Driving with others	Chauffeuring kids to activities and friends' homes	30 min/day x 6 days/week = 3 hours	120
Driving solo	Shopping, visiting friends	1 hour	30
Bicycling	Recreation	2 hours	20
Airplane travel	Two pleasure trips per year	30 hours per year	18,000 per year

NOTES

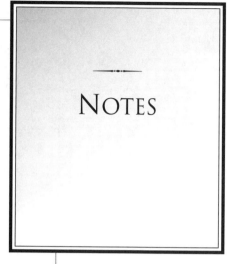

INTRODUCTION

1. For information on existing simplicity study circles and groups, log on to The Simple Living Network [www.simpleliving.net].

LESSON 1

1. National Association of Home Builders [www.nahb.org], citing US Census Bureau.
2. U.S. Department of Commerce, *National Income and Product Accounts*, 2002.
3. National Opinion Research Center, University of Chicago.
4. Juliet B. Schor, *The Overworked American: The Unexpected Decline of Leisure* (New York: BasicBooks, 1991), pp. 28–32.
5. Based on a study conducted by the International Labour Organization, as reported in the *World of Work*, September/October, 1999.
6. For a comprehensive review of research studies on happiness, see Tim Kasser, *The High Price of Materialism* (Boston: MIT Press, 2002) and David G. Myers, *The Pursuit of Happiness: Discovering the Pathway to Fulfillment, Well-Being, and Enduring Personal Joy* (New York: William Morrow, 1992).
7. Seth Dunn and Christopher Flavin, "Moving the Climate Change Agenda Forward," *State of the World 2002* (New York: W.W. Norton, 2002), p. 34.
8. United Nations Human Development Report 1998, *Consumption for Human Development* (New York: 1998).

LESSON 2

1. The source of all data about Mall of America is its web site [www.mallofamerica.com].
2. As reported in *Sierra* (January/February 2003), magazine of the Sierra Club.

LESSON 3

1. See Tim Kasser, *The High Price of Materialism* (Boston: MIT Press, 2002) and David G. Myers, *The Pursuit of Happiness: Discovering the Pathway to Fulfillment, Well-Being, and Enduring Personal Joy* (New York: William Morrow, 1992).
2. See Juliet B. Schor, *The Overspent American: Why We Want What We Don't Need* (New York: HarperCollins, 1999) pp. 11–19.

3. American Cancer Society [www.cancer.org].
4. Statistical Abstract of the United States, 2001.
5. Ibid.
6. Ibid.
7. Ibid.

LESSON 4

1. National Association of Home Builders [www.nahb.org], citing US Census Bureau data.
2. "Housing Statistics in the European Union 2002," a report published by the Department of Housing of the Direction General of Planning, Housing and Heritage, Belgium, p. 25.
3. US Census Bureau, *Demographic Trends in the 20th Century*, reports a decrease from 3.38 people per household in 1950 to 2.59 people per household in 2000.
4. National Association of Home Builders [www.nahb.org].
5. The Associated Press with Richard Williams, "Restless Americans Move Frequently," *Amarillo Globe-News Business Writer*, October, 1998, citing the U.S. Census Bureau.
6. PBS, "The First Measured Century" by Host/Essayist Ben Wattenberg, citing *This U.S.A.: An Unexpected Family Portrait of 194,067,296 Americans Drawn from the Census* (New York: Doubleday, 1965); Mark Baldassare, "Suburban Communities," *Annual Review of Sociology* 18 (1992): 475–494; U.S. Census Bureau.
7. The Congress for New Urbanism [www.cnu.org], a trade association for architects, planners, builders, and developers, is an excellent resource for the New Urbanism movement. Their web site includes a database of new urbanist communities. See also the Smart Growth Network [www.smartgrowth.org] and Smart Growth America [www.smartgrowthamerica.org].

LESSON 5

1. Schor, *The Overworked American*, pp. 28-32.
2. *Yearning for Balance*, 1995 report prepared by the Harvard Group for the Merck Family Fund. Also, 1997 survey by the Families and Work Institute in New York found that 64 percent of employees said they would like to work fewer hours, up from 47 percent in 1992. Source: Wall Street Journal, January 17, 2001.
3. Schor, *The Overworked American*, pp. 28–32.

4. *World of Work* magazine, No. 31, September / October 1999, International Labour Organization.
5. James Lardner, "World-class Workaholics," *U.S. News & World Report*, December 13, 1999.
6. *World of Work* magazine, No. 31, September / October 1999, International Labour Organization.
7. Schor, *The Overworked American*, pp. 128–132.
8. Anders Hayden, *Sharing the Work, Sparing the Planet: Work Time, Consumption, & Ecology* (London: Zed Books, 2000), p. 62.
9. The Take Back Your Time campaign [www.timeday.org] is sponsored by The Simplicity Forum [www.simplicityforum.org], an international alliance of leaders committed to achieving and honoring simple, just, and sustainable ways of life. John de Graaf, PBS producer of the Affluenza series, is spearheading this campaign.

LESSON 6

1. *Statistical Abstract of the United States*, 2001, Table # 579.
2. This profile is evident in the results of The Pierce Simplicity Study (less than 10 out of 211 people would qualify as a mainstream drop-out) as well as in a review of the popular books on simplicity.
3. See "Pessimism for the Future," by Nancy McCarthy, *California Bar Journal*, November, 1994.
4. Statistics on self-employment were obtained from reports of the U.S. Department of Labor, Bureau of Labor Statistics.
5. Hayden, *Sharing the Work, Sparing the Planet*, p. 35.
6. Schor, *The Overworked American*, p. 2.

LESSON 7

1. John de Graaf, David Wann, and Thomas H. Naylor. *Affluenza: The All-Consuming Epidemic* (San Francisco: Berrett-Koehler, 2001), p. 89.
2. Molly O'Meara Sheehan, *City Limits: Putting Brakes on Sprawl*, Worldwatch Paper 156 (Worldwatch Institute, 2001), p. 11; Lester R. Brown, *Eco-Economy: Building an Economy for the Earth* (New York: W.W. Norton, 2001), p. 201.
3. Brown, *Eco-Economy*, p. 193, citing A Texas Transportation Institute Study, 2001.
4. Ibid., p. 188.

5. Ibid., p. 200.
6. Ibid., p. 206.
7. See the Car Sharing Network [www.carsharing.net].
8. Brown, *Eco-Economy*, p. 201.
9. Lisa Mastny, "Redirecting International Tourism," *State of the World 2002* (New York: W. W. Norton, 2002), p. 105.
10. World Tourism Organization, a United Nations intergovernmental organization of 139 countries, January 27, 2003 press release.
11. Mastny, "Redirecting International Tourism," p. 120.

LESSON 9

1. See, for example, a study authored by Kenneth Mukamal of Beth Israel Deaconess Medical Center in Boston, as reported in the *New England Journal of Medicine*, January 9, 2003.
2. Richard Carmona, U.S. Surgeon General, press conference on January 22, 2003, as reported in *The Orlando Sentinel.*
3. U.S. Surgeon General, "Physical Activity and Health" report, 1996.
4. Brown, *Eco-Economy*, p. 146, citing estimates from Worldwatch Institute and U.N. Food and Agricultural Organization.
5. Estimates provided by The Hunger Project, a non-profit organization founded in 1977, based on data from UNICEF; "The State of Food Insecurity in the World 2002," a report of U.N. Food and Agricultural Organization (as to number of deaths of children under five).
6. "Reducing Poverty and Hunger: The Critical Role for Financing for Food, Agriculture and Rural Development, 2002," p. 12 (paper prepared by the Food and Agricultural Organization, International Fund for Agricultural Development and World Food Programme, all U.N. agencies); U.N. Food and Agricultural Organization Report, 1998 Statistics; see also Frances Moore Lappé and Anna Lappé, *Hope's Edge: The Next Diet for a Small Planet* (New York: Tarcher/Putnam, 2002), p. 15
7. Mathis Wackernagel and William Rees, *Our Ecological Footprint: Reducing Human Impact on Earth* (Gabriola Island, B.C.: New Society Publishers, 1996), p. 13.
8. The Worldwatch Institute, *State of the World 2002* (New York: W.W. Norton, 2002), p. 56; "Reducing Poverty and Hunger: The Critical Role for Financing for Food, Agriculture and Rural Development, 2002," p. 11 (paper prepared by Food and Agricul-

tural Organization, International Fund for Agricultural Development and World Food Programme, all U.N. agencies).

9. UNAIDS, "Aids Epidemic Update 2002" p. 34.

LESSON 10

1. Regarding time spent by children, structured sports doubled from 2 hours, 20 minutes per week to 5 hours, 17 minutes per week and studying increased by nearly 50 percent from 1981 to 1997. Sandra L. Hofferth, "Changes in American Children's Time, 1981–1997," University of Michigan's Institute for Social Research, Center Survey, January, 1999.
2. Hofferth, "Changes in American Children's Time, 1981–1997."
3. RGA Communications, The 1995 Kentucky Fried Chicken Family Dinner Survey.

CHAPTER 12

1. Brown, *Eco-Economy*, p. 50.
2. Chris Bright, "A History of Our Future," State of the World 2003 (New York: W.W. Norton, 2003), p. 5.
3. Sandra Postel, Pillar of Sand: Can the Irrigation Miracle Last? (New York: W.W. Norton, 1999), p. 255.
4. Bright, "A History of Our Future," p. 5.
5. Ibid.
6. Emily Matthews, et al., *Pilot Analysis of Global Ecosystems: Forest Ecosystems* (Washington, D.C.: World Resources Institute, 2000) pp. 3, 16.
7. The U.N. Food and Agriculture Organization (FAO), *Global Forest Resource Assessment 2000* (Rome: 2001).
8. Bright, "A History of Our Future," p. 8.
9. The U.N. Food and Agriculture Organization (FAO), *The State of World Fisheries and Aquaculture 2000* (Rome: 2000).
10. Robert Engelman, Brian Halweil, and Danielle Nierenberg, "Rethinking Population, Improving Lives," *State of the World 2002* (New York: W.W. Norton, 2002) p. 129.
11. United Nations Human Development Report 1998, *Consumption for Human Development* (New York: 1998), p. 50.
12. Janet Sawin, "Charting a New Energy Future," *State of the World 2003* (New York: W.W. Norton, 2003), p. 88, citing the U.N. Framework Convention on Climate Change (UNFCCC).
13. Wackernagel and Rees, *Our Ecological Footprint*, p. 13.

14. John Robbins, *The Food Revolution: How Your Diet Can Help Save Your Life and Our World* (Berkeley: Conari Press, 2001), p. 293.
15. The U.N. Food and Agriculture Organization (FAO), *Yield Response to Water* (Rome: 1979).
16. Hayden, *Sharing the Work, Sparing the Planet*, p. 13, citing the World Commission on Environment and Development, *Our Common Future*, pp. 22–23.
17. Brown, *Eco-Economy*, pp. 12–13.

BIBLIOGRAPHY

Andrews, Cecile. *Circle of Simplicity: Return to the Good Life.* New York: Harper Collins, 1997.

Aslett, Don. *Clutter's Last Stand: It's Time to De-Junk Your Life.* Cincinnati: Writer's Digest Books, 1984.

Bender, Sue. *Plain & Simple: A Woman's Journey to the Amish.* New York: Harper, 1989.

Bennett, Hal Zina and Sparrow, Susan J. *Follow Your Bliss.* Upper Lake, CA: Tenacity Press, 1997.

Bennett, Hal Zina. *Write from the Heart: Unleashing the Power of Your Creativity.* Novato, CA: New World Library, 2nd edition, 2001.

Berry, Wendell. *The Unsettling of America: Culture & Agriculture.* San Francisco: Sierra Club, 3rd edition, 1996.

Berthold-Bond, Annie. *Better Basics for the Home: Simple Solutions for Less Toxic Living.* New York: Three Rivers Press, 1999.

Blix, Jacqueline and Heitmiller, David. *Getting a Life: Strategies for Simple Living Based on the Revolutionary Program for Financial Freedom from Your Money or Your Life.* New York: Viking Penguin, Revised 1999.

Bobel, Chris. *The Paradox of Natural Mothering.* Philadelphia: Temple University Press, 2001.

Boldt, Laurence G. *How to Find the Work You Love.* New York: Arkana, 1996.

Breathnach, Sarah Ban. *Simple Abundance: A Daybook of Comfort and* Joy. New York: Warner, 1995.

Briskin, Alan. *The Stirring of the Soul in the Workplace.* San Francisco: Berrett-Koehler, Reprinted 1998.

Brown, Lester R. *Eco-Economy: Building an Economy for the Earth.* New York: W.W. Norton, 2001.

Burch, Mark A. *Simplicity: Notes, Stories and Exercises for Developing Unimaginable Wealth.* Gabriola Island, B.C.: New Society Publishers, 1995.

———. *Stepping Lightly: Simplicity for People and the Planet.* Gabriola Island, B.C.: New Society Publishers, 2000.

Cameron, Julia. *The Artist's Way: A Spiritual Path to Higher Creativity.* New York: J.P. Tarcher, 10th edition, 2002.

Campbell, Jeff. *Clutter Control: Putting Your Home on a Diet.* New York: Dell Publishing, 1992.

Czech, Brian. *Shoveling Fuel for a Runaway Train: Errant Economists, Shameful Spenders, and a Plan to Stop Them All.* Berkeley: University of California Press, 2000.

Cox, Connie and Evatt, Cris. *30 Days to a Simpler Life*. New York: The Penguin Group, 1998.

Dacyczn, Amy. *The Complete Tightwad Gazette: Promoting Thrift as a Viable Alternative Lifestyle*. New York: Random House, 1999.

Dappen, Andy. *Shattering the Two-Income Myth: Daily Secrets for Living Well on One Income*. Mountlake Terrace, WA: Brier Books, 1997.

Davidson, Jeff. *Breathing Space: Living and Working at a Comfortable Pace in a Sped-Up Society*. Chapel Hill, NC: Breathing Space Institute, Revised 2000.

de Graaf, John and Wann, David and Naylor, Thomas H. *Affluenza: The All-Consuming Epidemic*. San Francisco: Berrett-Koehler, 2001.

de Graaf, John (ed.). *Take Back Your Time*. San Francisco: Berrett-Koehler, September, 2003.

Dlugozima, Hope and Scott, James and Sharp, David. *Six Months Off: How to Plan, Negotiate, and Take the Break You Need without Burning Bridges or Going Broke*. New York: Henry Holt, 1996.

Doherty, William and Carlson, Barbara. *Putting Family First: Successful Strategies for Reclaiming Family Life in a Hurry-Up World*. New York: Owl Books, 2002.

Dominguez, Joe and Robin, Vicki. *Your Money or Your Life: Transforming Your Relationship with Money and Achieving Financial Independence*. New York: Penguin Books, Revised 1999.

Drake, John D. *Downshifting: How to Work Less and Enjoy Life More*. San Francisco: Berrett-Koehler, 2001.

Duany, Andres and Plater-Zyberk, Elizabeth and Speck, Jeff. *Suburban Nation: The Rise of Sprawl and the Decline of the American Dream*. New York: North Point Press, 2001.

Durning, Alan. *How Much is Enough?: The Consumer Society and the Future of the Earth*. New York: W.W. Norton, 1992.

Edwards, Paul and Edwards, Sarah. *Working from Home: Everything You Need to Know about Living and Working under the Same Roof*. New York: J.P. Tarcher, 5th edition, 1999.

Elgin, Duane. *Promise Ahead: A Vision of Hope and Action for Humanity's Future*. New York: Quill, 2001.

———. *Voluntary Simplicity: Toward a Way of Life that is Outwardly Simple, Inwardly Rich*. New York: Quill, Revised 1993.

Fogler, Michael. *Un-Jobbing: The Adult Liberation Handbook*. Lexington, KY: Free Choice Press, 2nd edition, 1999.

Foster, Richard J. *Freedom of Simplicity*. New York: Harper, 1998.

Fromm, Erich. *To Have or To Be?* New York: Continuum, Reissued 1996.

Fox, Matthew. *The Reinvention of Work: A New Vision of Livelihood for Our Time*. New York: Harper San Francisco, 1995.

Gregg, Richard. *The Value of Voluntary Simplicity*. Wallingford, PA: Pendle Hill, 1936.

Hall, Colin and Lieber, Ron. *Taking Time Off: Inspiring Stories of Students Who Enjoyed Successful Breaks from College and How You Can Plan Your Own*. New York: Noonday Press, 1996.

Hawken, Paul and Lovins, Amory and Lovins, L. Hunter. *Natural Capitalism: Creating the Next Industrial Revolution*. New York: Back Bay Books, 2000.

Hayden, Anders. *Sharing the Work, Sparing the Planet: Work Time, Consumption, & Ecology*. London: Zed Books, 2000.

Hochschild, Arlie Russell. *The Time Bind: When Work Becomes Home and Home Becomes Work*. New York: Owl Books, Reissued 2001.

Kabat-Zinn, Jon. *Wherever You Go There You Are: Mindfulness Meditation in Everyday Life*. New York: Hyperion, 1994.

Kasser, Tim. *The High Price of Materialism*. Boston: MIT Press, 2002.

Keeva, Steven. *Transforming Practices: Finding Joy and Satisfaction in the Legal Life*. Chicago: McGraw Hill/Contemporary Books, 1999.

Lappé, Frances Moore and Lappé, Anna. *Hope's Edge: The Next Diet for a Small Planet*. New York: J.P. Tarcher, 2002.

Lara, Adair. *Slowing Down in a Speeded Up World*. Berkeley: Conari Press, 1994.

Lazear, Jonathon. *The Man Who Mistook His Job for a Life: A Chronic Overachiever Finds the Way Home*. New York: Crown Publishers, 2001.

Levering, Frank and Urbanska, Wanda. *Simple Living: One Couple's Search for a Better Life*. New York: Viking Penguin, 1992.

Lindbergh, Anne Morrow. *Gift From the Sea*. New York: Pantheon Books, Reissued 1991.

Lippe, Toinette. *Nothing Left Over: A Plain and Simple Life*. New York: J. P. Tarcher, 2002.

Lockwood, Georgene. *Complete Idiot's Guide to Simple Living*. Indianapolis, IN: Alpha Books, 2000.

Long, Charles. *How to Survive Without a Salary: Learning to Live the Conserver Lifestyle*. Toronto: Warwick Publishing, Revised 1996.

Longacre, Doris Janzen. *Living More with Less*. Scottdale, PA: Herald Press, 1980.

Lotter, Donald W. *EarthScore: Your Personal Environmental Audit & Guide*. Lafayette, CA: Morning Sun Press, 1993.

Luhrs, Janet. *The Simple Living Guide: A Sourcebook for Less Stressful, More Joyful Living*. New York: Broadway Books, 1997.

———. *Simple Loving: A Path to Deeper, More Sustainable Relationships*. New York: Penguin, 2000.

Maté, Ferenc. *A Reasonable Life: Toward a Simpler, Secure, More Humane Existence*. Pflugerville, TX: Albatross Publishing, 2nd edition, 2000.

McCamant, Kathryn and Durrett, Charles R. *Cohousing: A Contemporary Approach to Housing Ourselves*. Berkeley: Ten Speed Press, 2nd edition, 1993.

McCoy, Jonni. *Miserly Moms: Living on One Income in a Two-Income Economy*. Minneapolis, MN: Bethany House, 3rd edition, 2001.

McKenna, Elizabeth Perle. *When Work Doesn't Work Anymore: Women, Work, and Identity*. New York: Bantam Doubleday Dell, 1998.

Meadows, Donella H. and Meadows, Dennis L. and Randers, Jøgern. *Beyond the Limits: Confronting Global Collapse, Envisioning A Sustainable Future*. Post Mills, VT: Chelsea Green Publishing, Reprint 1993.

Michael, Michele. *The New Apartment Book*. New York: Clarkson N. Potter, December 1996.

Miller, Ph.D., Timothy. *How to Want What You Have: Discovering the Magic and Grandeur of Ordinary Existence*. New York: Avon, 1996.

Mills, Stephanie. *Epicurean Simplicity*. Washington: Island Press/ Shearwater Books, 2002.

Moore, Thomas. *Care of the Soul: A Guide for Cultivating Depth and Sacredness in Everyday Life*. New York: Harper Perennial, Reprinted 1994.

Morgan, Marlo. *Mutant Message Down Under*. New York: HarperCollins, Reprinted 1995.

Nearing, Scott and Nearing, Helen. *The Good Life: Helen and Scott Nearing's Sixty Years of Self-Sufficient Living*. New York: Schocken Books, Reprinted 1990.

O'Neill, Jessie. *The Golden Ghetto: The Psychology of Affluence*. Milwaukee, WI: The Affluenza Project, 1997.

Pierce, Linda Breen. *Choosing Simplicity: Real People Finding Peace and Fulfillment in a Complex World*. Carmel, CA: Gallagher Press, 2000.

Princen, Thomas and Maniates, Michael and Conca, Ken (eds.). *Confronting Consumption*. Cambridge, MA: MIT Press, 2002.

Rechtschaffen M.D., Stephan. *Timeshifting: Creating More Time to Enjoy Your Life*. New York: Doubleday, 1997.

Reid, Lisa. *Raising Kids with Just a Little Cash*. Santa Fe, NM: Ferguson-Carol Publishers, 1996.

Robbins, John. *Diet for a New America: How Your Food Choices Affect Your Health, Happiness and the Future of Life on Earth*. Novato, CA: H J Kramer, 1998.

———. *The Food Revolution: How Your Diet Can Help Save Your Life and Our World*. Berkeley: Conari Press, 2001.

Robinson, Jo and Staeheli, Jean Coppock. *Unplug the Christmas Machine: A Complete Guide to Putting Love and Joy Back into the Season*. New York: Quill, Revised 1991.

Robinson, Joe. *Work to Live: The Guide to Getting a Life*. New York: Perigee, 2003.

Ryan, John C. and Durning, Alan. *Stuff: The Secret Lives of Everyday Things*. Seattle: Northwest Environment Watch, 1997.

Schor, Juliet B. *The Overspent American: Why We Want What We Don't Need*. New York: HarperCollins, 1999.

———. *The Overworked American: The Unexpected Decline of Leisure*. New York: BasicBooks, Reprinted 1993.

Schut, Michael (ed.). *Simpler Living, Compassionate Life: A Christian Perspective*. Denver, CO: Living the Good News, 1999.

Schumacher, E.F. *Small is Beautiful: Economics as if People Mattered: 25 Years Later . . . With Commentaries*. Point Roberts, WA: Hartley & Marks, 2nd edition, 1999 (first published in 1973).

Segal, Jerome M. *Graceful Simplicity: Toward a Philosophy and Politics of Simple Living*. New York: Henry Holt, 1999.

Sherlock, Marie. *Living Simply With Children: A Voluntary Simplicity Guide: For Moms, Dads, and Kids Who Want to Reclaim the Bliss of Childhood and the Joy of Parenting*. New York: Three Rivers Press, 2003.

Shi, David E. *The Simple Life: Plain Living and High Thinking in American Culture*. Athens, GA: Univ of Georgia Press, Reprinted 2001.

Sinetar, Marsha. *Do What You Love, The Money Will Follow: Discovering Your Right Livelihood*. New York: Bantam Doubleday Dell, Reissued 1989.

———. *Ordinary People as Monks and Mystics: Lifestyles for Self-discovery*. New York: Paulist Press, 1986.

St. James, Elaine. *Inner Simplicity: 100 Ways to Regain Peace and Nourish Your Soul*. New York: Hyperion, 1995.

———. *Simplify Your Life: 100 Ways to Slow Down and Enjoy the Things That Really Matter*. New York: Hyperion, 1994.

———. *Simplify Your Work Life: Ways to Change the Way You Work So You Have More Time to Live*. New York: Hyperion, 2001.

St. James, Elaine and Cole, Vera. *Simplify Your Life with Kids: 100*

Ways to Make Family Life Easier and More Fun. Kansas City, MO: Andrews McMeel Publishing, 2000.

Susanka, Sarah. *The Not So Big House: A Blueprint for the Way We Really Live*. Newtown, CT: The Taunton Press, 1998.

Tatelbaum, Linda. *Carrying Water as a Way of Life: A Homesteader's History*. Appleton, ME: About Time Press, 1997.

Taylor, Betsy. *What Kids Really Want That Money Can't Buy*. New York: Warner Books, 2003.

Thomas, Kim. *Simplicity: Finding Peace by Uncluttering Your Life*. Nashville, TN: Broadman & Holman, 1999.

Thoreau, Henry David. *Walden and Other Writings*. New York: Modern Library, 2000.

Urbanska, Wanda and Levering, Frank. *Moving to a Small Town: A Guidebook for Moving from Urban to Rural America*. New York: Simon & Schuster, 1996.

Wackernagel, Mathis and Rees, William E. *Our Ecological Footprint: Reducing Human Impact on the Earth*. Gabriola Island, B.C.: New Society Publishers, 1995.

White, K.C. *Lilabean: A Story of Simplicity for Grown-up Girls*. Elizabeth City, NC: Bean Pot Press, 2002.

Whitmire, Catherine. *Plain Living: A Quaker Path to Simplicity*. Notre Dame, IN: Sorin Books, 2001.

Winter, Barbara J. *Making a Living Without a Job: Winning Ways for Creating Work that You Love*. New York: Bantam Doubleday Dell, 1993.

Zalewski, Angie and Ricks, Deana. *Cheap Talk with the Frugal Friends: Over 600 Tips, Tricks, and Creative Ideas for Saving Money*. Lancaster, PA: Starburst Publishers, 2001.

Zelinski, Ernie. *The Joy of Not Working: A Book for the Retired, Unemployed, and Overworked*. Berkeley: Ten Speed Press, 3rd edition, 1997.

Index

R

S

T

U

V

W

Y

Z

Choosing Simplicity

Real People Finding Peace and Fulfillment in a Complex World

(Gallagher Press, 2000, ISBN 0-9672067-1-5)

by Linda Breen Pierce

This groundbreaking work goes beyond the questions of *why to simplify* and *how to simplify* your life. This is the book that tells all–what has really happened in the lives of real people who have done it. What does simplicity look like in our modern, complex world? Can people who embrace this lifestyle sustain it over time? What are the downsides? Is it worth it? Do they miss the "old way?"

These are just a few of the questions explored by Linda Breen Pierce in *Choosing Simplicity*. Pierce spent three years studying people who have simplified their lives–over 200 people from 40 states and eight countries–people who live in the country, in large cities, and everywhere in between.

Interwoven throughout the stories are the author's reflections and insights, which offer guidance and support for those who want to explore simplicity in their own lives.

> "You are in for a treat. The stories in this book are rich in texture and color, the warp on which you will find yourself weaving reflections about your own life."
>
> —Vicki Robin, coauthor of *Your Money or Your Life*, from the Foreword to *Choosing Simplicity*

> "Linda Breen Pierce brings home the importance of the personal story. Reading the stories of the people in her study is liberating and exhilarating!"
>
> —Cecile Andrews, author of *Circle of Simplicity*

> "Linda Breen Pierce brings clarity and compassion to an insider's report on the simple life."
>
> —Duane Elgin, author of *Voluntary Simplicity* and *Promise Ahead*

> "People often ask me, 'Is it *really* possible to simplify your life?' The real life stories in *Choosing Simplicity* prove that it *is* possible. This book is an inspiration and guide for anyone who wants to live more simply."
>
> —Elaine St. James, author of *Simplify Your Life* and *Inner Simplicity*

PHOTO BY TOM O'NEAL PHOTOGRAPHY, CARMEL, CA

About the Author

Linda Breen Pierce once lived the so-called American dream. She earned a six-figure income as an attorney, wore expensive silk suits, and spent her vacations at lavish resorts. But after practicing law for 10 years, she realized that what she was giving to live this dream was not for sale.

Starting in 1991, Linda and her husband, Jim, proceeded to simplify their lives. They moved from Los Angeles to the Monterey Peninsula in central California. They downsized their housing to half their former space without feeling deprived in any way. While living on considerably less income, Linda and Jim now enjoy life much more than in their previous lifestyle of high-pressure work in large cities.

Linda no longer practices law. Writing and speaking on simplicity are her passions. Hiking, reading, and foreign travel are Linda's favorite leisure activities.

In 1996, Linda commenced a three-year research project known as *The Pierce Simplicity Study*. She studied the lives of over 200 people who live simply—people from 40 states and eight countries. She shares the results of this study and the inspiring stories of the study participants in her book, *Choosing Simplicity: Real People Finding Peace and Fulfillment in a Complex World*.

Linda is a founding member of *The Simplicity Forum*, a think tank and activist group of simplicity leaders. She created and maintains a web site called *The Simplicity Resource Guide* [www.gallagherpress.com/pierce], offering resources on voluntary simplicity and simple living.

Linda is also an international speaker and workshop leader on voluntary simplicity. For further information about Linda's speaking services, see www.gallagherpress.com/speaking.htm or contact Linda directly at pierce@gallagherpress.com.